PRAISE FOR *BETTER PLACES*

The world needs more books like this: books that share the journey to self-management and radical collaboration from the inside, books that give us a behind-the-scenes look at the hard process of unlearning a paradigm of zero-sum competition while building up a new way of seeing the world and the possibilities for a better way to work and live. Robert's story shines with authenticity and vulnerability and weaves together a personal history of tragedy and triumph with a bevy of cross-cultural insights that few of us will ever experience for ourselves—which is exactly why this book is so valuable, and so very needed in the world today.

—Matt K. Parker
Author, A Radical Enterprise

Robert and his company have won awards for achieving the "holy grail" of workplace culture: becoming a place where diverse people thrive. So many companies and CEOs aim to build transformational organizations, and Robert has done that. His stories, global citizenship, humanity, and compassion shine through in this book, which is a must-read for today's leaders. Those who pay attention to the learning inside these pages will have the edge as we face the future of work.

—Wendy Horng Brawer
Partner and head of innovation and learning, Intune Collective

Robert's personal journey and experiences provide valuable insights into building better places through compassion, authenticity, and nonviolent communication. The stories shared in *Better Places*, along with practical advice and lessons learned, offer a road map for creating positive change in our communities and workplaces. This book is a must-read for anyone seeking to transform their leadership style and build more compassionate and inclusive environments.

—Traci Walker
Executive director, Digital Services Coalition

Robert Rasmussen's book takes you on an inspiring, surprising journey. His own remarkable story is one thread—of traumatic beginnings, healing found in the kind, collective culture of Norway, and a wise, successful return to his home country of America. Robert weaves his tale together with lessons from key psychologists and organizational thinkers and includes a stirring account of improved government service as well as the almost-too-good-to-be-true saga of his IT firm, Agile Six. But it *is* true that he cofounded a firm based on compassion and a commitment to help employees grow into their most authentic selves—a firm that is highly profitable even though it focuses on people and purpose first. The end result is that you truly travel to a new state of mind—one convinced that *Better Places* to work are both desperately needed and entirely possible.

—Ed Frauenheim
Coauthor, A Great Place to Work for All *and* Reinventing Masculinity: The Liberating Power of Compassion and Connection

Better Places is essential reading for leaders aiming to foster environments where authentic collaboration happens and individuals flourish. I've been researching companies on the cutting edge of effective, human-centered organizations for almost a decade. Robert presents a captivating narrative on the transformative power of compassion and community-building. *Better Places* serves as a guiding light for those in search of genuine, purpose-oriented workplaces and communities. Robert dares to challenge conventional leadership norms by championing self-management, inclusion, and prioritizing purpose over profits and in doing so illuminates the transformative possibilities of an abundance mindset.

—Travis Marsh
Cofounder, Human First Works, trainer, and coach

BETTER PLACES

BETTER PLACES

BUILDING STRONGER COMMUNITIES WITH AUTHENTICITY AND COMPASSION

ROBERT RASMUSSEN

Advantage | Books

Published by Advantage Books, Charleston, South Carolina.
An imprint of Advantage Media.

ADVANTAGE is a registered trademark, and the Advantage colophon is a trademark of Advantage Media Group, Inc.

Printed in the United States of America.

10 9 8 7 6 5 4 3 2 1

ISBN: 978-1-64225-905-6 (Paperback)
ISBN: 978-1-64225-904-9 (eBook)

Library of Congress Control Number: 2024909318

Cover design by Lance Buckley.
Layout design by Ruthie Wood.

This publication is designed to provide accurate and authoritative information in regard to the subject matter covered. It is sold with the understanding that the publisher is not engaged in rendering legal, accounting, or other professional services. If legal advice or other expert assistance is required, the services of a competent professional person should be sought.

Advantage Books is an imprint of Advantage Media Group. Advantage Media helps busy entrepreneurs, CEOs, and leaders write and publish a book to grow their business and become the authority in their field. Advantage authors comprise an exclusive community of industry professionals, idea-makers, and thought leaders. For more information go to **advantagemedia.com**.

This book is dedicated with love to my late mother, Cheryl. Everyone in this world deserves to be loved, and she earned more than I was able to give.

And to my dear wife, Åse Lill, who taught me everything I know about this topic.

And to my late Uncle Robert, who authentically saw and valued every human who crossed his path.

CONTENTS

FOREWORD

Five years ago, I became a partner in a prestigious civil rights law firm. To get there, I spent fourteen years studying, outlining, writing briefs late into the night, and reviewing thousands of pages of discovery. So why did I decide to change course only one year later?

While disgruntled lawyers flee the legal profession in droves, I loved many parts of my job, particularly my diverse client base. My firm trusted me immensely, letting me work reduced hours, set my own schedule, and run my own cases. I eventually made partner while working part time, an accomplishment I had been told was impossible.

But achieving the impossible came at a cost. Under the guise that my job and clients required my all, I rescheduled my days off to make deadlines and attend meetings and court proceedings. Insecure about my part-time status, I felt obligated not only to work as hard as my colleagues but also to be available to jump into any situation. In addition, I learned quickly that doing all the things was not enough—I needed also to exude confidence in my ability to do them; that is, to balance work and home life.

Behind the confident exterior, I was tired. Parenting three young children, even with a spouse committed to an equal partnership, meant I carried a tremendous mental and physical load. I tried to equally prioritize my family and my work, but that elusive "balance" always seemed just out of reach. Instead, I went home drained, feeling each day as though I had left a small piece of myself at the office.

Every now and then, I would rejuvenate by taking long walks through the woods with my brother, Dan. Having built a successful career in digital contracting, first at the government and then on the outside, he both shared my passion for meaningful work and understood the struggle for balance.

He would listen patiently while I bemoaned my failure to have it all before enthusiastically explaining the changes Agile Six and other like-minded companies were driving within civic tech. He urged me to consider that this industry, which paired human-centered design with modern technology to improve the delivery of government services, may satisfy my needs for both meaningful work and balance.

Truth is, I was not convinced. While Dan's passion lies in the purpose of his work, mine is in the way we work. I knew his work was deeply purposeful, but so was my work at the firm. What I was missing was a collaborative, supportive team free from hierarchy. I was ready to leave the rat race. I did not know whether Agile Six would bring that change, but because I respected and admired Dan, I considered the possibility. Even if my goal felt different from what he promised, I decided to accept an interview to join Agile Six as general counsel.

I showed up to meet with Robert Rasmussen in a suit, notes prepared, ready to sell my broad experience in employment law and explain how I would overcome my knowledge void in government contracting. Robert, sitting casually in his T-shirt, dismissed my efforts to prove my qualifications. He trusted I was enough from before we even met—not because I was Dan's sister but because for Robert, trust is assumed and given freely.

He explained that he created Agile Six so that he could be the same person at home and at work after previous jobs forced him to be more than one person and severely damaged his mental health. He shared his dream of a workplace where colleagues supported one another in building great products, shared the results of their success, and went home to their families more energized and fulfilled from their efforts.

By extending an offer, he invited me to build this dream with him. I was intrigued and honored—what he promised seemed too good to be true. If I didn't have Dan vouching for Robert and the company, I probably would have walked away, laughing at the naivety of their dreams. At that time, I can't say I trusted as freely as Robert, but I trusted my brother, so I decided to become a Sixer.

In the five years since that interview, I have had the good fortune of working closely with Robert. In that time, the only constant has been reinventing how we work to prioritize our core values of purpose, wholeness, trust, self-management, and inclusion. He has pushed us to try new ideas and take on new challenges, such as establishing unlimited wellness time for employees and eliminating middle management and salary negotiation. We have debated, collaborated, experimented, and deconstructed. Significantly, I, too, have learned to trust our colleagues completely.

In the manifestation of Robert's dream, I found what I was searching for—a team that values our collective wholeness above individual success. I would love to say that having found that, I am no longer stressed about the demands of being a working parent. Of course, I can't. Like most of us, I still live under a tremendous mental and physical load. But here is what I can say: now, I feel secure admitting that I can't do it all and that when hard choices must be made, I choose to prioritize my family. I no longer pretend that I have a work meeting if I must pick up a sick child; when I take days off to go on field trips with my children, I proudly post pictures the next day in my work Slack.

And there is also this: I no longer leave work feeling like I have left a piece of myself behind. In embracing my wholeness, I have replaced my desire to climb the ladder with a deep humility and gratitude for our human collective, faith in people, and trust that what we give each day is enough. So strong is what we have built from Robert's vision that I now occasionally take it for granted, forgetting that many in the workforce still pretend that they can be everything to everyone, as they spend their days in sterile office spaces, competing for raises, interrupting their vacations for "urgent" work meetings, brainstorming prizes and awards to motivate subordinates, and navigating ways to win their boss's favor.

Thanks to Robert's leadership, I now believe in better places—places where we are encouraged to bring our whole selves, embrace our vulnerabilities, trust our colleagues, and prioritize the things that truly matter to us. In these places, we believe that we each want to contribute and know how much we can give, and we don't push our colleagues to give more. When someone needs the day off, we don't ask why. We make decisions based on who is most informed rather than hierarchies and seek the advice of our peers rather than a manager's approval. Crucially, we have one another's backs even if we disagree with their decision.

Robert has taught me that it is up to us to build these places but that to do so, we must trust one another enough to admit our vulnerabilities and honor our wholeness before all else. Just as my time working with Robert has changed my life, I am confident that this book will also change yours. Turn the page and join us in building better places.

—Emily Levenson, Esq.
Chief people officer and general counsel, Agile Six

PREFACE

Nonviolent Communication is based on the principle of Ahimsa—the natural state of compassion when no violence is present in the heart.

—MARSHALL ROSENBERG, FOUNDER OF THE CENTER FOR NONVIOLENT COMMUNICATION (CNVC)

What follows is my story. I pass it on to the reader for whatever lessons that you may take from it. I hope the case I make is that better places can exist. Life is not a contest of winners and losers; the sooner we push away from the competitive game of life, the sooner we can begin living the lives we are meant to live. Everyone, everywhere, is born into this world with a unique set of gifts to unfold upon it. The world suffers when we neglect to offer them up.

Better places, including those I have found abroad and those I have created here at home, embrace compassion and authenticity both individually and in collectives. Everyone is a winner in these willfully interdependent communities. Bad things still happen, needs go unmet, and pain is present. But where politics, individualism, humiliation, and competition wane, compassion and authenticity grow so that we can endure what hurts us together and share what brings us joy so that happiness is amplified.

If life was a zero-sum game of losers and winners, then I'd have to count myself as a loser. I was raised with unattainable standards, to believe winners matter more than losers, that second place is the first loser, and that life is a competition. But being the best at anything requires support I was not given. I was a survivor.

> AHIMSA IS THE HIGHEST DHARMA, AHIMSA IS THE HIGHEST SELF-CONTROL,
> AHIMSA IS THE GREATEST GIFT, AHIMSA IS THE BEST PRACTICE,
> AHIMSA IS THE HIGHEST SACRIFICE, AHIMSA IS THE FINEST STRENGTH,
> AHIMSA IS THE GREATEST FRIEND, AHIMSA IS THE GREATEST HAPPINESS,
> AHIMSA IS THE HIGHEST TRUTH, AND AHIMSA IS THE GREATEST TEACHING.
>
> —MAHABHARATA

Ahimsa is a Sanskrit word observed in the religions of Hinduism, Jainism, and Buddhism. It communicates the principle of nonviolence, of causing no harm to other living things. In this season of my life, it has been a transcendent intention, and I hope it is reflected in this book.

In the following chapters, I will share my journey toward compassion and authenticity, the lessons I have learned, and the tools that helped me along the way. With these lessons and tools, I have learned to process my life with grace for those I have loved, even through seasons of pain and discomfort. Among the tools I have found most useful are Nonviolence and Nonviolent Communication (NVC), Humanism, and Humanistic Psychology, Willful Interdependence, Teal/Evolutionary Culture, and most important, good, old-fashioned faith in people.

I have found that most pain and joy are relational to other human beings. We all exist to love and serve one another, and yet modern American society has evolved a language that is egoic, competitive, and violent. Our words have so much more impact on violence in the world than I ever understood, and our words, spoken or unspoken, profoundly influence our hearts, actions, and others. They set off unintentional and uncontrollable judgments, which, in turn, spark cycles of actual violence in the world.

Taken together, I hope my story will ease someone's journey and accelerate their authentic unfolding. The lesson is not to end disagreements but rather to adopt an outlook focused on increasing empathy and improving relationships.

We all have heard or echoed the common playground taunt: *Sticks and stones may break my bones, but words will never hurt me.* Nothing is further from the truth. Occasionally, in a supermarket or restaurant, I hear the scowl of an impatient parent who has lost control. I try not to judge people the way many judged my own mother who acted this way often. Still, I feel the pain of children imposed by those they love and trust most, and I must intentionally contain myself not to step in.

Why do we act in ways that injure those we love the most? Why has our language evolved so maliciously? A monster lives inside all of us. It rises in the very short moment between perception and reaction when we feel judged or humiliated, and then ego seizes control of the undisciplined mind to strike back, to inflict humiliation upon someone else.

Marshal Rosenberg referred to this judgment-based tendency as Jackal Language.[1] I will borrow and personify that metaphor. This Jackal is the undisciplined fragile ego that passes self-judgment in all words and situations. The Jackal is the voice of the humiliated ego, doing everything it can to avoid further humiliation. It rewards us with labels, loser or winner; either is unhealthy. If we don't learn to manage it, it has the power to destroy. This judgmental voice lives in me still and surprises me when it hops out without permission to undermine my self-worth or the safety, esteem, and joy of those I love.

Jackals lived unchecked within my childhood family. We yelled a lot in our home and somehow accepted it as our culture. It is true; we got better at living with monsters—or so I once thought. Others would see the Jackals around the house, and I would say, "It's just how we communicate; it's meant with love."[2]

But Jackals do not know unconditional love; they never coexist. I meet various versions of Jackals in people all the time, and lest you feel superior, I assure you that it lives in you also. If you feed it, it will grow; if you starve it, it will hide, waiting for the next opportunity to emerge. But it is rarely silent. It feeds on our innermost thoughts and self-judgment. It absorbs our self-compassion and then empathy for others.

And our American culture is built around its assessments. A winner-take-all culture rewards the Jackal and often brutally punishes the humble. We are either the humiliators or humiliated; those are the options. Consider the posters, T-shirts, bumper stickers, and speech of our political parties. They motivate us to polls out of retribution and fear of humiliation, and our "'team'" must be victorious, and too often our policies and values end up on the back seat.

The purpose of this book is to share the lessons I have learned to produce the truly remarkable communities I celebrate. The one thing they all have in common is that they involve authentic expression of authentic compassion—voices louder than Jackals. Voices of joy, fellowship, and abundance. These are not perfect communities, but they are willfully interdependent, endeavoring to feed one another and transcend the harsh, extrinsically driven appetites of a competitive and highly individualistic culture.

I hope that sharing the news of their success will inspire people to build communities of their own, including workplaces and educational institutions where people can unfold more organically.

VISIT MY BLOG AT WWW.BETTERPLACES.BLOG FOR MORE ENGAGING STORIES AND INSIGHTS ON CREATING BETTER PLACES.

INTRODUCTION

As soon as men live entirely in accord with the law of love natural to their hearts and now revealed to them, which excludes all resistance by violence, and therefore hold aloof from all participation in violence— as soon as this happens, not only will hundreds be unable to enslave millions, but not even millions will be able to enslave a single individual.

—LEO TOLSTOY

Since you have picked up my book, I want to thank you for your patience. I am not a writer by trade, and much of what I will share is personal. As I write this, I am mindful of my privilege and struggles. I never want to be ungrateful for either. What I have learned and applied in my life has been borne out of fear, insecurity, and unmet needs but thrives more often now in joy, abundance, and love.

The first story I share is my typical "pick yourself up by your own bootstraps" story. I intend to tell it with humility and gratitude for all the people and circumstances that changed my life. I intend to take all the risks and be vulnerable. My personal definition of leadership is to go into unsafe spaces and make them safe for others to enter.

As for everyone else involved, you, the reader, the family members or friends who will come up, and the communities that supported me, I want you to feel safe. All of you, my *village*, deserve the credit for my journey. This is where I intend my storytelling to be different. You see, it was not my own bootstraps, after all; you and many others picked me up, and this book is for you.

My father was very passionate; he had profound things to say his whole life. He could have been better at small talk but was always ready to debate or discuss the meaning of life. He was not perfect; in fact, he was deeply flawed. But so am I. While the content of my message is different from his, I still recognize his passion in the mirror. His message and mine also have many similarities: *life is sacred; live it, embrace it, be present for others now, and be ready when your name is called to leave.*

Dad was a self-proclaimed biblical literalist and apologetic. A "Bible Christian," he believed there were no mistakes in the inspired Word of God, and he was happy to sit with anyone for hours to defend it. But even as a child, I sensed a contradiction between what the Bible said, as interpreted by my parent's actions, and what Jesus said about the unconditional love of children.

In Matthew 18:4, Jesus calls them the "greatest" in the Kingdom. But in Jesus's times, children were not treated thus. We see this in Matthew 19 and Luke 18 when parents were bringing their infants to be blessed by Jesus, and the disciples tried to chase them away. In their opinion, the Lord had more important things to do.

I experienced the eighties much the same way. Trust was earned, and love was conditioned upon obedience, performance, and the appropriate level of repentance. I remember my parents loved *The Cosby Show*. My mother's favorite quote was from the first episode when the titular character tells his son, "I brought you into the world;

I can take you out."[3] This was funny, I am sure, to many. But to me, it was echoed amid violence from my mother along with the biblical authority she derived from Proverbs 13:24 instructing her not to "spare the rod," which empowered her parental authority to inflict violence in her states of anger.

My father studied the scriptures most of his life as a layman. He was ordained in his late sixties after losing his mobility, sight, and much of his hearing. Still, he spent every Sunday at Sunridge Village Assisted Living Center, preaching to his flock of thirty memory care patients. Despite all his flaws, he loved my mother without compromise. This is what brought a man with a near-perfect memory to reside in a memory care unit.

You see, as my mom declined into early-onset dementia, he insisted that we find a home where he could go with her. She passed away a few years after arriving, but his own declining health never allowed him the opportunity to leave. He had a photographic memory and would recite the Bible or quote the scholars from memories of the hundreds of books he had read over the years. It was hard to argue that God had not worked through him to bless these lonely people, nor that Pastor Jim did not love the calling even so late in his life.

I almost preceded Dad into the ministry. When I was very young, I studied in a Bible College for two years and entertained what I felt were callings. I recall one excellent professor named Dr. Lund, who set me straight on that.

"Robert," he said, "if you can resist the calling, it is not a true calling. God is not ambivalent; if you are called, then you will not be able to resist."

I would later read something akin to this from the humanist psychologist Abraham Maslow in an essay about what he called "Meta-motivation." Maslow describes it more like falling in love. He said there is a merger of what we need to do (external obligation) and what we want to do (intrinsic needs); when these two things are the same, we have our calling.[4]

As a religious person, I have experienced this feeling in church, and it has come and gone with the seasons of my life. But this book is not a religious book, and it is not about what I have learned in the church. It is about what I now feel is my calling to share what I have learned in my cultural travels—about how together, we can build better places through "willful interdependence," a term I hope will resonate as jumping, headfirst, into the collective arms of our communities. It means embracing compassion and authenticity and rejecting politics, individualism, humiliation, and competition.

I have fallen in love only once. I met a Norwegian woman named Åse Lill Frigstad in my second year of Bible studies. In her eyes, I saw unconditional love, which I had lacked. In her arms, I found my first home, and there was no ambivalence. It was what Dr. Lund and Dr. Maslow had described; what I wanted and needed to do was the same. My story will lead to our story, how we raised our children abroad, and how it molded me by stripping away the myth of independence. Most important, perhaps, is how with her, I unlearned the conditional love with which my parents raised me and ever since have been working to replace it with unconditional humanistic love.

The rest of this book is about how I received and applied that love to the world and all the truly unique things that came about. I hope you find something in my story that ignites or serves your calling.

I am an entrepreneur in the government technology space, and I will share that story as well. As my business has grown, I have been blessed to meet and recruit people who are more intelligent, younger, and better than I am. They have built upon my dreams a genuinely groundbreaking company, and now I am in a season where I can begin to transition the stewardship of these dreams to them. This affords me, among many luxuries, the ability to spend more time in Norway, a place that has shaped me and become a second home.

This book will encourage my two homes to learn from each other. To be honest, I think more lessons are directed to my American compatriots, something perhaps I can remedy in a future book.

CHAPTER ONE

TANGLED LINES

One of my favorite customs in Norway is *fellesferie*, which means "joint holiday." It is a time in summer when all Norwegians have the right to take a vacation simultaneously. This means most businesses are closed or operating under reduced hours, so people can reunite with loved ones in the brief summer sun.

At the invitation of my sister-in-law, we were recently able to spend time by the sea at a modest cabin on the Norwegian coast, packed close together with family, including adult nephews and nieces and their romantic partners. We went fishing, hiked, played board games, and spent time together.

One afternoon, the young adults went fishing alone and came home with a messy net of tangled fishing line. I have seen many tangled lines, but this one was perhaps the worst. My brother-in-law Jonas and I saw a challenge, maybe a bonding opportunity, and used the next few days to take turns recovering the mess. If you know me, you know I love both fishing and a good metaphor. So, as I took my turn with this task, an analogy came to mind.

Any parent fishing with their children will likely have spent time untangling fishing lines. It is the instinct of new anglers when they meet a tangle to try to apply pressure and yank the line free. This often has the unfortunate outcome of turning a tangle into a tight knot and creating new tangles. As you struggle and pull, wild things may emerge. We instruct new anglers not to pull on the line; instead, slow down and begin to unravel the tangle carefully.

Our lives and our anxieties are much the same. The more we rush to pull on the line, judge others hastily, and allow perceived self-judgments to influence us, the tighter we pull these emotional knots. We quickly develop triggers that act like new tangles and become new knots when force is applied. And like a nylon fishing line, once a knot is removed, the line retains its memory, making it easier for knots to reform quickly.

Like a jerked response to a tangled line, violent communication, which is much of the topic of this book, introduces judgments, creates knots from simple tangles, and draws conflict based on the judgment of ourselves and others. Unfortunately, I learned this lesson a few years after my father passed away, when a friend introduced me to NVC and the work of Marshal Rosenberg. I wish I could have found this twenty years ago and used it to untangle the knots between me and my father. NVC immediately reshaped my relationships, first with myself and then with everyone around me. While I still live with "line memory," it has improved my life exponentially.

This book attempts to share the lessons I have learned to stop creating knots. As I write this, war has broken out again in the Middle East, persists in Ukraine, and over forty other armed conflicts rage to take lives around the world. We are tying ourselves in knots and attracting new tangles individually and as nations. It's time to stop pulling on the line.

I am someone who has experienced a lot of shifting. I have traveled geographically, having lived in Norway for over ten years and traveled the world for leisure, work, and military service. I have traveled philosophically as well. I am both a military Veteran and a pacifist. I have traveled economically, having experienced food and shelter insecurity and financial independence.

Sometimes it feels like I have traveled between worlds. I don't mean between dimensions or galaxies but worlds separated by fear, ego, or forces of bias handed down to us by thousands of years of evolution. And honestly, in a historically divided time, it seems more accessible to bridge dimensions or galaxies than simple ideologies. But on this journey, I have discovered bridges that link the worlds and the people that I love to each other.

My experiences have finally given me the mandate to share what I have learned. I am aware that my message meets the culture in a time of unrest and division. It will be tempting for some readers to place me with one side or the other in the context of current events or culture wars. But I humbly ask the reader to trust me and my intent. I mean only to share things I have come to believe sincerely. Having seen these ideas reshape the lives of families I care about, I feel obligated to share.

I know what I have learned and will share is not new thinking. But perhaps it will rekindle or remind you, the reader, that you are not as independent as you think you are, and in my world, you are not a loser, or a winner, but a precious and amazing creation called human. This message grew out of necessity in my heart as I struggled to mend fences. I would discover much of it in the work of two late psychologists, Dr. Abraham Maslow and Dr. Marshal Rosenberg, and this is reflected in my entire book. Maslow died in his early sixties, the year I was born and a short time before Rosenberg rose to prominence.

But I have wondered what the world would look like if these two humanist psychologists collaborated successfully. Their work teaches us how to untangle our lines without creating the knots. They teach us to cast our lines into more transcendent seas and catch what is truly alive in us and others. They help us to gratify ourselves and others and transcend judgment or humiliation, to unfold what the universe has put into us, individually and collectively. They are vital to the restoration of the individual and the American Dream.

Maslow's significant contribution, which most will recognize, was that all humans have everyday common needs and that these needs, once gratified, enable transcendence to higher-level needs. Rosenberg's work (NVC) teaches us how to recognize those needs in ourselves and others and how to gratify them without judgment. Those needs, unlike our Jackal judgments, are in fact universal and good. They are the same universal needs of any human, although they are wrapped up in different individual circumstances.

I have pleaded with everyone close to me to invest some time in reading Dr. Rosenberg's books, because seeing those needs and learning to meet them without judgment have changed my life in miraculous ways. Regarding the aforementioned metaphor, Maslow identified the tangles in our fishing line. Rosenberg helped us untangle them.

Both Rosenberg and Maslow had criticism for modern approaches to psychology and psychotherapy. I am not qualified to do more than echo those concerns. Still, I sense that we often go to professionals to help us untie the knots of anxiety in our lives even as we produce new ones. Instead, or at least in addition, we need to stop pulling on the line. Only once we do will we start to understand what is authentically alive within ourselves and others. And this takes constant practice, so many who pursue this course refer to it as a lifelong practice.

As a quick note, in this narrative, when I reference "violent," it's an encompassing term that replaces ambiguities like "toxic," "divisive," or "competitive." These words mask the truth that our linguistic choices can escalate tensions, stifling mutual compassion. The outcome of undisciplined words is almost always some degree of humiliation and violence. This book champions compassion, opposing coercive language that trades in fear, guilt, or shame. Every word, uttered or internalized, influences our mindset. This book's heart is a plea to see and understand each other honestly. Let's eradicate judgment, embrace empathy, and fundamentally reshape our interactions.

Why now? Recent societal shifts in the United States appear to signal a yearning for kinder, less combative communication. After navigating intense political divides and a relentless pandemic, there's a collective pivot toward a gentler perspective. Or at least that is what I hope.

Consider the meteoric rise of *Ted Lasso* on Apple TV. While its Emmy accolades highlight brilliant acting and scripting, the show's unique appeal lies in its titular character. With all his vulnerabilities, Coach Lasso radiates a transformative, nonviolent worldview. Despite insurmountable challenges and a world conspiring against him, his tenacious faith and humility shine. And like a contagion in response to his vision, an interdependent, multicultural collective evolves around him. His ethos resonates with many, especially those seeking sanctuary from ruthless workplaces.

Ted Lasso's leadership mirrors an essential truth: lasting change doesn't come from force but from unwavering belief and vulnerable submission to that belief. While the pandemic made businesses cede control, it unveiled an undeniable reality—trust isn't just a virtue; it's a necessity. As Ted's office sign proclaims, "Believe." In this context, "believing" means letting go, trusting, and embracing authenticity in the locker room, boardroom, and our living rooms. The echoes of this philosophy resonate in movements like Quiet Quitting and The Great Resignation. The message is clear and powerful: Stop pulling on the line. Trust people. They have earned it.

What does this mean for America?

Having spent time abroad, I am increasingly convinced that the whole world, and even more so, Americans, must learn to act and communicate more intentionally, collectively, and less violently. Particularly now and in the United States, we are tying ourselves in so many knots that it is increasingly complex to see a future together. Rarely a day passes that I do not daydream of leaving the United States to live once more among less violent people. I am sure that is as hard for the reader to hear as it is for me to admit.

As time passes, it becomes increasingly difficult to imagine a positive outcome in our community as the problems and obstacles continue to accumulate. We all have heard the idea that there is more that binds us than divides us. We need leaders who can act on this idea and build bridges to our commonalities.

We have done this at the company and the coalition I have built. We collectively have rejected the false narrative that our government must choose to be either more efficient or more effective. It can and must be both. To achieve that, we need to listen to one another without judgment, to truly hear and see first what is in ourselves authentically, and then what is in each other. We must stop pulling on the line and start sorting out the tangles in our democracy.

What follows are three stories about the bridges I have built to create better places. The first is about my journey from an underprivileged childhood to cofounding and growing a successful company, not simply in terms of profit but also, more important, of purpose, kindness, nonviolence, and love for our commonality.

The second story is about that company and how we reinvented corporate leadership by looking to foreign models, embracing humanism, egalitarianism, NVC, safety, inclusion, and the sense of wonderful community these things create.

The last story is a movement of companies and public servants in my industry, like-minded, embracing the same ideas to reshape how our employers and governments interact with people.

The intention of the company and coalition I founded was simple: stop blaming the politicians and fix this. The government "for the people, by the people" must be "of the people" once again.

We have already established that the purpose of this book is to create better places by embracing compassion and authenticity and rejecting politics, individualism, and competition. But now let's go a step further into how we get there. As we proceed, I would ask leaders to consider three new paradigms. These three ideas could change the world:

First, *bet the whole enchilada on people*. Stop pulling on the line. Trust people, and they will be trustworthy. Believe in them, and they will believe in themselves, put purpose before profit, and see how it maximizes both. Mind the lines for tangles and practice nonviolent communication. As you do, you will attract like-minded soulmates and feed their souls and families. Model balance and take vacations, and demand that others do as well. Hold space for emergence, unfolding, and dreaming; these things cannot manifest in unbalanced or violent workplaces. *Be vulnerable and love people, and they will do the same.* This is leadership.

Second, *expect more from your politicians, employers, and one another*. Accept nothing less than trust, purpose, autonomy, and wholeness. You can stop the cycle of judgments and ask for balance. If you want to realize your full potential, you must demand nothing less. I will tell the story of my compromise in this area, how it nearly killed me, and how it made every bit of difference when I demanded balance for myself first. You should be welcome to bring the fullness of your identity or all you are comfortable bringing to work. You should be able to express your humanity and unfold it, bring it home whole, and have the energy to share it even more with your family. This is the world we need to build; it is then the world *we need to demand*. Trust me—I did, and it made all the difference.

Finally, *embrace your countrymen as interdependent compatriots*. End the culture war. We have defined our culture as one of independence and freedom. But this is simply a cowboy fairytale. We swim in the same waters, we thrive in the same economy, we breathe the same air, and our grandchildren will suffer the same consequences of our division and individualism. I can tell you, as someone who lived ten years in a social democracy, we pay very similar taxes and get much less in return. This is not an argument for tax reform. This is an argument for heart reform. *That starts with willful and proud ownership of our interdependence.* A true patriot loves their country and their countrymen.

Now, more than ever, the world needs a new kind of leader who sees abundance and not scarcity, takes risks to question their conceptions, and dares to talk of love, belonging, esteem, wholeness, and transcendence. We desperately need these leaders in our government, classrooms, communities, and businesses to see what unites us, what is alive in us, and what needs to be unfolded, not tangled up.

CHAPTER TWO

ATTACHMENT ISSUES

When a child first catches adults out—when it first walks into his grave little head that adults do not have divine intelligence, that their judgments are not always wise, their thinking true, their sentences just— his world falls into panic desolation. The gods are fallen and all safety gone.

—JOHN STEINBECK, *EAST OF EDEN*

I mentioned in the introduction that I would be vulnerable. So, in this chapter, let me jump right in. I didn't come from privilege, self-confidence, a nurturing childhood, or even a pure work ethic. My success was a product of necessity—I needed to believe the world was more than a competition and sought to find that place.

I have met many wonderful, more privileged people in my career. Some have asked casual questions, like "Where did you go to college?" or "What sports did you play in high school?" These well-meaning people have caused me unintentional pain with these questions because high school was a dark time for me, and it is for many underprivileged kids. Extracurricular activities often take a back seat to survival. The narrative of the "glory days" of high school proms, football, and college visits is far from the focus for some.

That's why questions about my college background or high school experiences aren't just uncomfortable—they revive traumatic memories. Abraham Maslow described a hierarchy of needs. We first seek safety, food, love and belonging, esteem, and self-actualization.

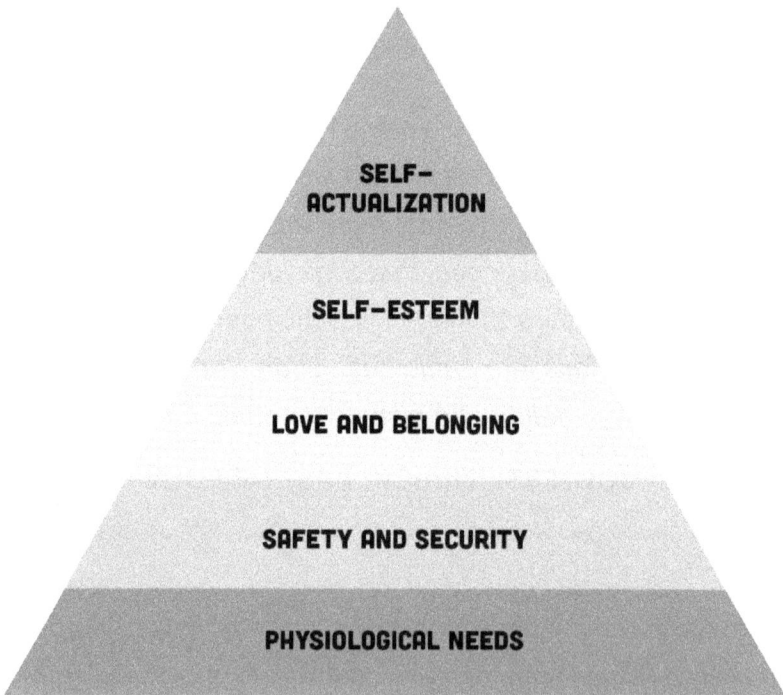

Saul McLeod, "Maslow's hierarchy of needs," illustration, Simply Psychology, last modified January 24, 2024, https://www.simplypsychology.org/maslow.html.

Attachment theory describes the process of how young children develop a relationship with at least one primary caregiver and from there learn how to negotiate needs with other humans. If a child lacks these, their future attachments and growth suffer. My childhood? I had a fractured bond with my mother early on, resulting in hardship for many years. For most of my developmental years, I had few if any successful attachments. So my needs went largely unmet. This chapter dives into how strong villages can step in where parents are unable.

My mother struggled with undiagnosed mental challenges, which I later suspected to be a mix of learning disabilities, childhood trauma, attachment disorder, and potential sociopathic tendencies. Developmentally challenged (perhaps at a twelve-year-old level in many ways) and traumatized, she treated her three boys in a childlike (detached) way, as possessions, toys to be picked up or put down as a child will treat a doll. Her longing for a daughter, our sister, lost shortly after birth, shattered her and any minimal attachments she had with me, and she passed this trauma on to her surviving children. She got very little, if any, psychological help following this tragedy.

My father's grieving strategy seemed to me to be evasive—ignore her issues and dive into other interests, work, televised sports, and church, leaving us often without his attention. He simply looked the other way. Violence, evictions, bankruptcy, and transient living marred our life at home.

We lived a nomadic life, evicted from several homes and relocating schools every eighteen months. In high school, all of this would come to a head. I had long outgrown my mother's intellect, and our relationship was strained by my young, irreverent banter and her propensity for anger and violence in response. Years later, it became clear that she couldn't love me in the traditional sense of a mother. I believe she suffered from an attachment neglect of her own as a child (or worse), leaving her without the instinct to navigate healthy attachments. Her unaddressed mental issues, developmental challenges, and my father's seeming indifference clouded my childhood in repression. I refuse to lay blame. However, I believe this chapter is crucial to understanding my journey.

With a record of evictions and judgments, we often landed in underprivileged and unsafe neighborhoods. In high school, our home was about three miles from campus, with several gang and crime zones between. Like many Los Angeles commuters, my father would drive up to two hours to get to work, so he dropped me off at school very early, often before five o'clock in the morning, having had no breakfast and carrying no lunch bag or lunch money. On my route home, I'd stray, finding myself in troublesome situations such as violent fights and shoplifting for food. I felt isolated, constantly shifting from one place to another because of my parents' unstable lifestyle. At school, I was the invisible kid no one cared to check on. At home, my father's apathy as we went hungry and were abused puzzled me. His inability or disinterest to protect me from harm was perplexing and hurtful.

In my first year, I failed most of my classes. My father's response was violent and unempathetic. Despite his own impoverished childhood, he had been an excellent student, and he could not understand how the fruit could fall so far from the tree. It was all my fault. And at that time, not knowing Maslow's work as I do now, I believed him.

FINDING MY COMMUNITY

My parents did put me in places where others could help. My extended family stepped up in the form of Dad's sister, Aunt Rose, and her husband, Uncle Robert. Dad's escape in the church became my escape as I dove into Boy Scouts and other extracurricular activities in our congregation. It was here I would start to build my village. My church friends Mathew and Jodi, whom I am still blessed to know almost like siblings, and their families became my other saving grace.

Still, every eighteen months or so, the world would blow up and strain all attachments I had created. For example, in the middle of my junior year of high school, just as I was starting to find a level of academic confidence, my family faced another financial crisis, leading us to move to a new community with a new high school further from our church. This transition was existentially risky, as it limited my access to the few social connections I had finally formed after years of difficulty. Fortunately, I had already obtained my driver's license, bought my first car, and was growing confident at school. Graduating from high school was a triumph, given my tumultuous journey. I was nearly last (if not last) in my graduating class and slightly surprised when they actually called my name to cross the stage. College seemed an unreachable dream until a door opened to a Bible College in Anaheim, California. The allure of escape was irresistible. My sanctuary? Once again, it was the church.

While my village nurtured my confidence, my parents, particularly my father, regularly thwarted it. Inside him lived a Jackal with a perfect memory and a vicious tongue. While my mother was physically abusive in her childlike state, my father was verbally gifted and sometimes cruel. My parents were both ill-equipped for their roles as they carried the generational trauma of poverty and abuse. Because she was born with developmental challenges, my mother could not be a mother. She did not have the tools to attach to her children and feed them, so I have forgiven her long ago.

In writing this book, I experienced more critical feelings for my father, who I am still working to forgive. In his defense, he is remembered by many as a giving and intelligent man. My best friends looked up to him as a mentor and model. He found time to teach Sunday school and lead youth groups. As much as all of this heartens me, it also confuses me. Even while mentoring my peers, he was often the enemy of my development. It was as if I was a source of humiliation where pride should live.

In my teens, my father seemed to sense my growing independence and the new relationships I formed with my church, jobs, and other extracurricular activities. Instead of encouraging these things, he used them as leverage, threatening to withhold access to them as punishment, often for not getting along with my abusive mother. As an adolescent and adult, he often would say, "Why can't you be more like your cousin?" Many years later, when I finally pieced together a part-time bachelor's degree, thanks to the G. I. Bill, his comment was, "That can't have been a hard program; I know what a weak student you are."

His words seemed rooted in a misconception of esteem as a zero-sum game, a contest to be won or lost, and we somehow were never on the same team. Any failure I had in life humiliated him, and any success I had threatened him. It was almost like we were siblings. Our attachment was not paternal care, or for the sake of meeting healthy and normal needs, but that of a rival to avoid or inflict humiliation. Or perhaps he saw me as a reflection of himself, and I did not measure up. I have come to understand that his words reflected wounds that went untreated, attachments broken in his own life. We never learned to feed each other, so we fed on each other.

We would outgrow this odd disposition only after my mother passed, and he found himself feeble, blind, and living in an assisted living center. You could say he was humbled by life and where the ego gave up, grace came in. And in that brief time we shared tender, authentic moments. I think it is the normal life cycle of attachment that we feed our children until it's their turn to renegotiate the attachment so that they can feed us in old age. So instead of my father becoming my child (which is a more natural progression), my sibling became my child.

In retrospect, it had much to do with his insecurities about the abundance of esteem, perhaps from losing his own mother at a tender age and having to take her place as the parent to his own siblings. Esteem was something I would have given him in abundance if he could ask.

From my village, however, I was shown kindness, fed, and recognized for my worth, particularly by my church friend Mat's parents, Dick and Nancy, and by my Aunt Rose and Uncle Robert. I met my Aunt Rose and Uncle Robert when I was about five years old and attached to them as if they were my own parents. This was a critical saving grace in my life. Finally I had someone to care about me, even if it was at a distance. Rose became my mother, something that I dearly needed, but it only exacerbated the tensions with my birth mom who often fiercely resented our relationship. Their voices and actions countered those of my father; their homes were always welcoming, and their pantries stocked. These acts sowed the seeds of a community that would be my lifeline and unfold eventually as my life's mission. I fear I can never thank them enough.

When a road resembling college (Bible school) materialized at seventeen years old, the only ambition that truly motivated me was to escape my childhood home, so I ran for it. More church people—heck yes! But it was a refuge more than an education, and I met many other refugees at Bible school, including my wife. They are still some of my favorite people in the world.

The love I found by chance outside of the home may have turned me from a drain on society to a successful entrepreneur, a creator of jobs, and a taxpayer. Like someone who has escaped a burning building, it seems critical now for me to advocate for this business case. As a society, we need to spend resources on feeding, sheltering, and protecting children, breaking the cycle of insecurity and not incarcerating the products of insecure homes and unhealthy attachments.

We should not hope that children stumble upon a kind village. Our public schools should offer every child the support they need to break this cycle. This targeted support has the potential to turn many traumatized children into healthy tax-paying citizens and compassionate parents. As we mold the next generation, we must ensure that every young soul, regardless of background and environment, has multiple redundant opportunities to attach humanely, build self-esteem and peace, and thrive, not just survive.

Often, as was eventually my case, these young people are also easy prey for military recruiters. Although this can be a positive development, it seems unfair in the world's most prosperous country to ask underprivileged or unprepared teenagers to risk their lives for basic needs. Many enlist out of duty alone, but I think this number is fewer than we like to admit. I strongly believe that, like me, many enlisted warriors enter the service with post-traumatic stress induced by detachment, poverty, and violence, which is then compounded by the experiences we encounter while serving. We must recognize and rectify the inadequacies of systems that marginalize rather than uplift children and young adults.

A few years ago, my first cousin, best friend, and closest confidant, Ernie, Aunt Rose's son, said something to me that unexpectedly shook me. With tremendous respect, he said, "Robert, I saw what you went through; I have seen what you have done with your life; if you can do it, anyone can." Ernie was by no means overly privileged either, and while he had a better situation in some regards than I had, he also worked harder than anyone I knew. This comment went a long way to motivating me to share my story because, while I appreciate the compliment, no child should have to "do it." We should not celebrate the self-reliance and survival of a child. Children should not need to find their own bootstraps.

CHAPTER THREE

AUTHENTICITY

I believe that before all else I am a reasonable human being, just as you are—or, at all events, that I must try and become one.

—HENRIK IBSEN, *THE DOLL'S HOUSE: A PLAY*

I was sure of a few things when I graduated from Bible College: I was going to marry that Norwegian girl, and I was not going to be a pastor. Beyond that, I needed more answers. I mentioned earlier that people like me are easy prey for military recruiters, and I was really excited about the original *Top Gun* movie. After studying aviation for a semester in junior college, it was easy for a Navy recruiter to convince me to enlist with the promise that I could work with jets and earn enough to pay for college while simultaneously supporting a young family.

When Åse Lill's student journey ended, we got engaged. She was surprised to learn I enlisted before she could voice an opposition. Looking back, she would have been justified if she had been enraged at my ambition, which ended up leaving her alone, eventually with a young daughter, for months at a time while I was repeatedly deployed. But she had no idea what we were getting into. Neither did I.

The Navy was the first time in my life that I could occupationally focus. Throughout high school and Bible school, I worked multiple jobs. I never realized my academic potential. My first job in the Navy was that of an aircraft mechanic, and my first assignment after boot camp was to the aviation training facility in Millington, Tennessee. No one told me precisely what an "unaccompanied assignment" was, so I showed up in Millington with my new bride in tow.

I'll always remember our first night experience as we arrived in the middle of the base late on a Friday night with suitcases in the rain and no place to sleep. The usual routine was for bachelors and unaccompanied men to check into the bachelors' barracks. Instead, we headed to the Navy Lodge (a hotel specifically for traveling military) on base and got a room. We found a small trailer the next day off base that would be our first "home" as a couple.

Having my wife around during that summer of training would provide a significant advantage as we had been studying partners in Bible school; she was a great help! The course was nine weeks long and very competitive. A lot was on the line for such a short course. Students would pick their ultimate duty assignments by academic rank. The choice of duty assignments was significant as it could mean sea or shore duty and the port of our choice. The highest-achieving student would be immediately promoted to petty officer (from pay grade E1–E4). So, on the table that summer was the potential to avoid the separation of deployment and the poverty of junior enlistment. The other students had no chance!

My wife and I studied all summer with the ambition of young lovers intent on not being separated. I found my academic potential for the first time and finished first in my class. Unfortunately, when the list of duty assignments arrived, all of them were sea duty tours. So, I would head out to the fleet as a young petty officer, and my wife would establish a home life in a foreign country without me. Our life in the Navy was not easy. Pay sucked, and we were separated for almost half of my first enlistment (twenty-two out of forty-eight months). We did get to choose locations, and San Diego was our first choice. Still, the neighborhood we could afford was unsafe, and I can only imagine how scary it was for my wife to live alone when I was deployed.

Fortunately, the military is an excellent source of community, and we made friends there that could only be the product of shared sacrifice. I thrived professionally as I donned a clean, fresh uniform that would hide any history of poverty or failure. For the first time in my life, I was with peers and treated as an equal. When I enlisted at the Military Enlistment Processing Center in Los Angeles, I met people of all backgrounds and economic levels. I have often wondered if some of them, who were people from other racial backgrounds, enjoyed the same refuge I felt when donning the Navy blues.

After my first enlistment of four years, I decided that aviation was not my thing. I had grown very excited about the advent of the personal computer and the internet. So, I reenlisted to learn information technology. I had also asked for guaranteed shore duty so that I would not have to leave my family again. Our daughter had arrived by this time, so we were a small family. After career retraining in information technology, we were sent to Oakland, California.

Even in 1998, the Bay Area was expensive, so we eventually bought our first home in a suburb of Sacramento, over 100 miles away from work. I would spend these three years completing a bachelor's degree in the evenings and commuting two hours each way to work.

I would drive pizzas part time to pay for gifts during the holidays. Our second child, Kevin, arrived during that season, and my wife and I served as youth pastors in our local church. Even as I write this, I don't understand how we did so much with our time. There was not much sleep.

But it all paid off! I finished my second enlistment just as the dot-com bubble was at its peak, and there was plenty of opportunity for systems engineers. We headed back to San Diego, and my civilian career got off to a great start. A few years later, after a season of head-hunters calling the house, I casually asked my wife, "What should we ask for?" Her response would change everything: "Well, if I could have anything, I would like to go home to Norway."

CHAPTER FOUR

WILLFUL INTERDEPENDENCE (COLLECTIVE ATTACHMENT)

The task that remains is to cope with our interdependence—to see ourselves reflected in every other human being and to respect and honor our differences.

—MELBA PATTILLO BEALS

Where parents fail, society can step in. Children can attach to community resources like the Boys and Girls Clubs, youth groups, and scouts. And societies can offer collective support to meet material needs. When I first landed in Norway, my upbringing—conditioned to never take healthcare, safety, or shelter for granted—made me wary of what I initially saw as socialism. At first, I resisted their way of life, even as its essence took root within me. Over time, my perspective shifted. I saw the benefits and advantages of this way of life. I began to appreciate the value of a society prioritizing collective well-being, enabling its citizens, particularly children, to focus on realizing their true potential. Ensuring everyone's basic needs are met allows individuals to evolve, pursue their passions, and grow without being constantly burdened by existential fears. Contrary to what many economic theories preach, and at the risk of being redundant, I'm convinced that such societal investments not only recoup their costs but also foster a generation of innovators, entrepreneurs, and responsible citizens.

The work culture in Norway did not immediately resonate with me. I recall a medical screening on the first day of my new position at Ericsson (the large telecommunications firm). I took the doctor's message to me as naïve. As I recall, it was something like this: "Robert," he said. "I know you are driven and knowing you are American, I imagine you work hard. But please, let me know if things get hard; at any point, if you feel like you are not comfortable or need a break, call me, and I can send you home."

I have grown to appreciate this attitude, and it's very close to a policy we have at my company, Agile Six. We call them Wellness Days (as opposed to the more negative term "Sick Days") and sometimes refer to them simply as "Nope Days" as in, "Nope, I can't do this today." Unlike many firms with traditional sick-day policies, we set no limit on Wellness Days and require no management or doctor's approval. We trust instead that our colleagues want to do great work from a place of wholeness and will do so as they are able. We trust them. In return, they get their work done. We have very low turnover and very satisfied clients.

While this is radical thinking by some American corporate standards, it was a standard in Norway that professionals were trusted by default. The supportive social net also meant that the consequences of unemployment did not induce as much existential fear. I remember thinking, "This can't work!" And wondering, "Why do people work when they really don't have to?"

I discovered a fundamental but profound reason for this. People are purpose-driven creatures. All things being equal, when people are healthy and supported, they want to work, and they yearn to contribute, to express their value to the world and to feel seen, heard, and valued in return, something Maslow referred to as "meta-motivation."[5] He created this term to describe the motivation of people who are self-actualized and striving beyond the scope of their basic needs to reach their full potential. As a skeptic, I often watched national unemployment and gross domestic product figures in Norway and the United States, looking for a "gotcha" moment. While these figures are hard to compare in differing systems, they consistently supported the idea that working less (or less triggered) produced more.

Another lesson is summed up by the common phrase, "We work to live, not live to work." I heard this on many occasions as my Norwegian colleagues practically sat on me with love, as they attempted to convince me that I had more to offer the world than only my professional ambition. Workdays were enforced at 7.5 hours, including two coffee breaks and lunch; we all did these ceremonies together. Initially, I would attempt to work through coffee or leave half an hour late. One by one, colleagues would file past my office, "Coffee break, Robert, we all go," or "Time to go home, we'll be back tomorrow!" I fictitiously wonder if they had some kind of secret meetings together, coordinating this approach to managing "the American."

I remember thinking at first that this was a "blue-collar" attitude, a distinction I also would learn was not really a part of Norwegian lexicon. Balance, wholeness, and work-life boundaries were not the sole rights of the nonexempt employee; they were the cultural norm or rule, even if there were exceptions in some companies (I suspect especially in American-owned companies). And there was little or no distinction between the "workers" in blue collars and the "professionals" in white collars. Both were to be valued, trusted, esteemed, and protected.

Understanding how humans serve needs and unfold meaning was the business case for those "nope days" mentioned earlier. These "higher needs" are the raw materials of inspiration and better products and services. If and when we are not well, not feeling safe, not feeling loved, not feeling whole, we are not nearly as effective, and we may even be counterproductive to others with whom we work. Showing up well is critical to creating great ideas, products, and teams.

As the years passed in Norway, I found myself experiencing more and more happiness. I learned to respect the customs, and I noticed that my colleagues were terrific stewards of the benefits and autonomy we were given. More importantly, they were compassionate stewards of one another's well-being and of my well-being. We had little demand of our managers as we took great care of one another. We were willfully interdependent.

I was still more ambitious than most, and I climbed a small career ladder I later realized was created intentionally by my leadership to satisfy my American appetites (maybe discussed at those secret meetings?). But inside me, my ego rebelled regularly against the "easy" life. Eventually, my ego and the ambitions drilled into me as a child reared up to take it away. Perhaps it can be called a midlife crisis. I was frustrated by comparing my career trajectory and the careers of my former American peers on LinkedIn. I was approaching forty, and I needed to prove myself.

In 2010, after nine years of shelter at Ericsson, I stupidly accepted an offer from an American firm in Boston to serve as their program director for northern Europe. They needed someone in the region with experience like mine, and they needed someone quickly. I needed a fancy title and pay raise to assuage my ego. The job was everything I wanted and nothing I needed. They paid me nearly double what I had received at Ericsson.

But they needed me fast because they had projects all over Europe that were in existential crisis. My typical weekly schedule included a Monday morning drive four hours from my home to a client in Oslo, then a flight to Copenhagen to meet a client there, a train to Amsterdam on Tuesday morning, Brussels on Wednesday, and back to Amsterdam before heading home on Friday! The travel routine was fun at first. But the job itself, combined with the travel, nearly killed me. I had four major programs in these four cities, all with local teams staffed from Ukraine or Russia. The staff were all away from home and struggling with their own language and cultural barriers. As I understood, neither the Norwegian rules nor those of the host countries applied to our teams. My job was to travel around and "motivate" them, and motivation was fear-based—something my years in Norway had left me ill-prepared me to do.

Navigating multiple demanding projects, I often stepped into roles beyond my expertise, driven by a need to salvage faltering client relationships. The ambiguity in company culture, shifting hierarchies, and my employer's evident indifference toward me left me perpetually on edge. I was constantly adapting, juggling multiple personas— whether I was a stern boss or a caring vendor—across four countries every week. When I returned home, the dissonance was jarring. Which of these versions was the real me? None of them.

This relentless pace and an eroding sense of self took a toll on my health, spiraling me into obesity, alcohol dependence, and an inactive lifestyle. One morning, haunted by persistent chest pains, I was convinced I was having a heart attack. But the emergency room unveiled a different truth: panic attacks. These bouts of anxiety, characterized by a profound dread sensation, began dominating my life. Conversations with others made it clear that this wasn't unique to me—many grapple with this overwhelming feeling of losing oneself. Every facade I adopted amplified this anxiety.

In this crucible of emotional turmoil, I had an epiphany. The dissonance, the dread—it all stemmed from being inauthentic. This revelation was both a curse and a blessing. From that point, I vowed to be true to myself, casting away all masks. I sought wholeness, believing it to be a fundamental yet often overlooked human need. I recognize now that this tumultuous period was a prelude, guiding me toward unfolding a greater purpose back home. And that would eventually lead me to the creation of Agile Six.

CHAPTER FIVE

THE SCANDINAVIAN MODEL

Two things define you: your patience when you have nothing and your attitude when you have everything.

—IMAM ALI

When I think of happy people, I think of Denmark. Despite having perhaps the highest taxes in the world, Denmark often tops the list of the World Happiness Report.[6] Danes reinvest up to half their income in tax and then face a 25 percent value-added tax on most items.[7] Most of their neighbors, who have similarly challenging weather, isolation, and taxation, are in the top ten of the ranking.[8] What have they got to be so happy about?

I have had the tremendous pleasure of working with many Danes while abroad. You will undoubtedly hear them complain about their government as well and even, on occasion, yearn for some of our ideas. But in my experience (and it's borne out by international polls), they are complaining from a much happier place. How can it be that the highest-taxed people in the world are consistently ranked among the happiest?

> *IN DENMARK, FEW HAVE TOO MUCH, AND EVEN FEWER HAVE TOO LITTLE.*
> —NIKOLAI FREDERIK SEVERIN GRUNDTVIG, INFLUENTIAL DANISH THINKER AND PRIEST, 1820

Through my enriching experiences collaborating with Danes, I've observed a common thread—faith in their governance based on faith in one another. Amid political diversity and occasional grievances, the Danish have an inherent trust in one another. Their approach isn't just about bureaucracy; it's deeply humanistic, underscoring their holistic, collective mindset.

So, how do we build this thinking in the United States? It starts with showing people what their government can be, restoring trust and building hope. Every interaction with the government is an opportunity to rebuild its brand (incidentally, every election is an opportunity to hire a manager who believes in and will sell the brand as well). This high level of happiness is often attributed to several critical factors, including the country's solid social support systems, low levels of corruption, and the cultural values of hygge and the Law of Jante.

COZY COEXISTENCE—HYGGE

Hygge is a Danish word translated loosely but incompletely as "having fun" in English. It refers to the feeling of coziness and comfort that comes from being with loved ones and enjoying simple pleasures.[9]

This word is getting increasingly more attention globally as hygge design is characterized as a cozy twist on Scandinavian living that takes stock in simple pleasures. For me, it's about creating a warm and inviting atmosphere and taking the time to appreciate the good things in life, not only with our own family or friends but also at a societal level.

A very close verb I often encountered was *kose* in Norwegian, which strictly translates to "feeling cozy or comfortable."[10] The adjective form is *koselig*. Norwegian and Danish are almost identical in written form, and these two words are almost interchangeable in either language.

It was not uncommon for a meeting request from a colleague or client to include the terms; "it will be *koselig*." It struck me as odd when grown men would talk about "cozying" with one another at work or social events! But what they meant is not easily expressed in English; it means, in a sense, "Let's be intentional about the environment in which we meet. Let's invest in meeting in such a way that we keep things simple, create a nice informal atmosphere (perhaps with candles even and some nice fruit or chocolate), and it will be fun or *koselig*."

This intentionally noncompetitive and egalitarian spirit makes an excellent foundation for civil discussions about political differences, ideological ideas, and even sports, with less posturing and certainly less offense. I sense strongly that there is an underlining contract to a hygge moment in that participants are invested in one another, committed to civility and presence, and willfully interdependent. In support of this goal, most meeting rooms, offices, and public spaces in Norwegian buildings will include candles, cookies, coffee, and sometimes blankets.

The difference is evident in the political spectrum as well. For one thing, when one examines the population (in general) of the Norwegian Parliament versus the U.S. Congress, you may quickly notice that the Norwegian body is almost or approximately a reflection of society regarding female and minority representation, something that is more natural from a willfully interdependent perspective; we want one another to be represented because it protects the needs of each group.

While our leadership bodies (e.g., Congress) are often constructed of competitors like lawyers and businesspeople, their parliament is usually sourced from social services professionals, teachers, social workers, pastors, and environmentalists. This *koselig* environment often manifests in a higher level and more productive discourse. It is not unusual to see the opposition parties and governing leaders (even the prime minister) debating the merits of specific ideas on the evening TV programming and having lunch together in Oslo the next day. Imagine exchanging ideas based on merit and not on the deception of competitive politics or the ambition to humiliate others.

One of the critical reasons for the happiness of the Nordic countries is their emphasis on interdependence and egalitarian values. In 1973, when the international oil crisis limited the use of private cars, the late and beloved King Olav V traveled by public transport. In a well-known exchange, he was asked how he dared publicly go without bodyguards. He replied that he had four million bodyguards—the entire population of Norway. In times of trouble, people in these countries can rely on a robust social safety net to help them through difficult times. This includes things like universal healthcare, access to education, generous unemployment benefits, and other social welfare programs, but it also includes trust in one another. The result is that people in these countries are less likely to face financial insecurity and can feel more confident in their ability to cope with whatever life throws their way. Just like the investment of candles and cookies in the office meeting room, the society wants all its membership in general to interact from a place of comfort and security. Before a productive discourse can begin, first it must be *koselig*.

When I discuss the differences I see between Norway and the United States, I am also inclined to talk about egoic dispositions. I like to contrast common adages like "There is no second place," "Second place is first loser," or "Whatever you do, be the best." I was raised to define my self-worth compared with others and never settle for anything other than perfection (a standard I had never met). These approaches starkly contrast with more collective societies where self-worth is often a product of one's role in supporting the community, if not simply a given. How we show up together in these *koselig* or hygge places is also important, and much of that is best described as humble and collectively minded. This is reflected in something called the Law of Jante.

HUMILITY AS A PILLAR— THE LAW OF JANTE

The Law of Jante is a set of cultural norms that further emphasize the importance of humility and taking care of one another. This cultural emphasis on togetherness and community contributes to greater happiness and well-being. Here, the Law of Jante, deeply embedded in the Scandinavian psyche, plays a pivotal role. Originating from Aksel Sandemose's literary works, it champions humility and communal well-being over individual aggrandizement. It's not simply about suppressing ambition but rather promoting a communal version and harmony.

The Law of Jante consists of ten rules, which can be summarized as follows:[11]

1. DON'T THINK YOU ARE ANYTHING SPECIAL.

2. DON'T THINK YOU ARE AS GOOD AS US.

3. DON'T THINK YOU ARE SMARTER THAN US.

4. DON'T CONVINCE YOURSELF THAT YOU ARE BETTER THAN US.

5. DON'T THINK YOU KNOW MORE THAN US.

6. DON'T THINK YOU ARE MORE IMPORTANT THAN US.

7. DON'T THINK YOU ARE GOOD AT ANYTHING.

8. DON'T LAUGH AT US.

9. DON'T THINK ANYONE CARES ABOUT YOU.

10. DON'T THINK YOU CAN TEACH US ANYTHING.

Aksel Sandemose was a Danish-Norwegian writer and linguist best known for his novel, *A Fugitive Crosses His Tracks*, published in 1933, in which he introduced the concept quite accidentally. This novel tells the story of a man named Jens who is forced to flee his hometown after breaking these fictional town rules. While Sandemose's intention was critical of the Scandinavian values, it backfired by codifying the cultural norms in a way that came to represent them. For many, it empowered them to embrace these values.

Though obviously overstated for satirical sake, these rules are deeply ingrained in Scandinavian (and much of northern European) culture. I have heard many Scandinavians argue about the validity of these rules and to what extent they positively impact modern society.

Some Scandinavians agree with Sandemose. For example, they see a competitive disadvantage in humility. While I have seen and tried to mitigate the Law of Jante's influence on my own children (it caused some challenges landing jobs back in the United States), I have also grown to appreciate the upside. My children would never oversell their capabilities or discount someone else's. While this makes me proud, it leaves them often ill-equipped in the competitive world of American business.

And American business can also be ill-equipped to succeed in Scandinavia. One example involved the boardroom of a major Norwegian telecommunications firm. The firm had asked my company for a local program manager before hiring me, and I would soon see that the problem was one for Jante's Law. American firms tend to sell with irrational confidence. When I arrived, I encountered a struggling product implementation, a frustrated client, and an overconfident employer. The first few meetings with my counterpart went very well, and I found him more than forgiving of a few missed deadlines. I wondered what the problem was.

A meeting was set shortly after my arrival with some of the senior executives, and I would soon come to see it very clearly. A senior VP from my firm brought a very polished and confident sales deck to the meeting that communicated the value of our product, our vast experience globally, and some unrealistic promises. While this may have played very well in many cultures, the tone of the relationships sank. The customer did not want to know how innovative or out-standing our product was; they wanted us to show less confidence. They wanted the objective truth that we were a little over our heads and the vulnerable promise that we were committed to working with them toward a common outcome for as long as it took. It struck me so clearly that my colleagues were creating problems that even if their confidence had been merited, it would only disturb the hygge. Even as we were missing deadlines, the client served up warm coffee, candles, and cookies, while we, in return, answered with ego.

So, I immediately went to work teaching Norwegian-facing colleagues about Jante's Law and the value of shared humility. I suspect that lesson saved the relationship with this client and many northern European clients. The Law of Jante is applied beneficially by encouraging people to focus on community needs rather than on themselves and disjointed dependencies. In the case above, bragging about our prowess only served to turn an interdependent team environment into two independent teams: the client and ourselves. How can this serve anyone's interests? If the client allows you to be human, accept it! It's much harder to be Superman.

At a national level, humility helps foster community and belonging and promotes cooperation and collaboration among individuals. We should endeavor to meet our countrymen with a *koselig* spirit and with the humility of Jante. Where others struggle, we must recognize our own fortune and share it. We are interdependent; we cannot afford to neglect the underprivileged without amassing social debt (i.e., incarceration and crime). I know many Americans may see this as naïve, and I once did too.

There is a general understanding that I have encountered that everyone needs a hand occasionally; it's not something to be ashamed of; it's humanity. And according to Jante's Law, when it's my turn, there is no guilt in using the help.

THE PATH FORWARD

There's an underlying discontent, an unarticulated yearning many of us experience. This sensation, akin to a splinter in our minds, signals a more profound, systemic issue. To address it, we must reframe our perspectives, championing the collective over the individual, understanding that in the grand tapestry of life, we're all threads interconnected in intricate patterns. We must weave these threads with care, understanding, and love to truly thrive.

SEPTEMBER 11, 2001: AN AMERICAN ABROAD

Leadership is tested in the crucible of crisis, revealing the core of a nation's character. The early twenty-first century witnessed two seismic events in the United States and Norway—terrorist attacks that would forever alter the course of their respective histories. Through these events, the fabric of national resilience, unity, and vision were laid bare, exposing the profound differences in their responses and consequences.

Like most such events, people remember where they were on September 11, 2001. For my part, I had been in Norway for only a few months. I was sitting in an equipment lab receiving training as a new engineer. When the first plane hit the World Trade Center at 8:46 a.m. in New York, it would have been 2:46 p.m. in Norway, and we would have been wrapping up our day. The lab had a TV, so as events unfolded at about three o'clock in the afternoon, colleagues started heading into the room until it was rather crowded. I was the only American, and as soon as reality started sinking in, I felt my new colleagues glancing at me with empathy. There was not much time to rationalize the situation, as America was at war by the end of our shift at 3:30 p.m.

In the days that followed, my colleagues were very kind and conscientious. They would stop by my office to see how I was doing, offer condolences, and make sure I was well supported. Most Europeans reacted with sympathy as if to say we were all one Western community. But there were exceptions.

A week after the attacks, I found myself in an airport in Dublin where I overheard a couple of presumably Irish men casually commenting that "the Americans finally got what they deserved." I hesitate to tell that story because it was not the most prevalent opinion. Still, I do recall how safe they felt to have that discussion out loud in public. Looking back, it reminds me that trauma is not regarded as powerfully absent proximity. Watching your homeland deal with a major crisis from abroad is enlightening. This crisis would lead to two major wars in Iraq and Afghanistan and many casualties.

Readers may recall one reaction by President Bush that struck the world as particularly American; during a speech before Congress ten days after the attack, Mr. Bush had not perceived enough global support. "Every nation, in every region, now has a decision to make. Either you are with us, or you are with the terrorists,"[12] he said.

While I think most of the world could relate to Bush's anger over a perceived lack of solidarity, this statement probably played well with his growing nationalist base. But this was perceived by the Norwegians as simplistic, transactional, and bullish. It was also scarcity-minded. Often, numerous nuanced positions and potential options are lost in such a linear and limited assessment. Imposing these positions on potential partners likely only further damaged his support abroad. It was also a lost opportunity to lead Americans into a more abundant and nuanced assessment of global opinion and our values.

This idea is a recurring theme in the classic *Star Wars* stories. *In Episode III: Revenge of the Sith*, the emerging Sith Lord, Vader, declares a similar position before striking down his former mentor and friend.

ANAKIN: "IF YOU'RE NOT WITH ME, YOU'RE MY
ENEMY!"

OBI-WAN: "ONLY A SITH DEALS IN ABSOLUTES."

—STAR WARS: EPISODE III: REVENGE OF THE SITH

In the months and years that followed, my opinions of my culture and how it responded to this and other events would shift. I would find myself defending the actions of the Bush administration with my Norwegian friends and family and feeling more critical about them when spending time at home in the States. I do recall what I perceived as a sense of naivety in my Norwegian colleagues as they would say things like, "Nothing like this could ever happen in Norway." I wondered if that was true, and unfortunately, ten years later, we all would find out it was not.

LEADING WITH EMPATHY, NOT ANGER

The date July 22, 2011, will forever be etched in Norwegian memory. A twin terror attack—first, a bomb outside Prime Minister Jens Stoltenberg's office, followed by a mass shooting on Utøya Island—sent shock waves through the nation. The scale of the tragedy, the deadliest since World War II, was profound. It reached the corridors of power, affecting even those closest to the prime minister. The immediate question arose: Would Norway alter its foundational values in the face of terror?

Emerging from the chaos, Stoltenberg's response was a masterclass in empathetic leadership. Eschewing vengeance, he steered his nation toward a path of reflection and unity, urging "more democracy, more openness, and more humanity." Remarkably, Norway heeded the call. They didn't enact reactive policies or militarize their police. Instead, they doubled down on their commitment to an open, democratic society, culminating in the erection of a monument on Utøya Island—a symbol of their resilience and refusal to bow to fear.

> **WE ARE STILL SHOCKED BY WHAT HAS HAPPENED, BUT WE WILL NEVER GIVE UP OUR VALUES. OUR RESPONSE IS MORE DEMOCRACY, OPENNESS, AND HUMANITY.**
>
> **—JENS STOLTENBERG**

Ten years later, he gave another speech that began:

Today, we remember the 77 people brutally killed on July 22, 2011.
Eight of them in the government quarter in Oslo.
The heart of our democracy.
Men and women at the service of our country and its people.
Sixty-nine of them on the island of Utøya.
The future of democracy.
Young people gathered at a summer camp.
Together, they represented the will of the people in our open democratic system.
We miss them all.[13]

THE FUTURE WE CHOOSE

As someone who has lived in both countries, the divide is glaring. Bush's "us versus them" mentality sowed seeds for an escalating domestic culture war that still simmers today. It produced an unknowable number of ethical compromises, like those documented by American soldiers at Abu Ghraib. In contrast, Norway's leadership reinforced the best of their nature. Norway's choice to strengthen its core values underscores the power of leadership in shaping national destiny. Our leaders' choices can either cultivate a culture of fear and division or nurture one of empathy and unity. They can humanize, or they can dehumanize.

In conclusion, the tale of these two nations serves as a cautionary reflection for our global society. In our intricate, multifaceted world, the most influential leaders recognize the value of nuance, compassion, and unity, or they walk blindly down a road to violence. As the future unfolds, nations must decide which path to tread—the one of division and absolutism or the one of understanding and unity.

And so, as we stand at this crossroads, we must ask ourselves: Which path will we choose?

CHAPTER SIX

DELIVERING HAPPINESS

The thing to do, it seems to me, is to prepare yourself so you can be a rainbow in somebody else's cloud. Somebody who may not look like you. May not call God the same name you call God—if they call God at all. I may not dance your dances or speak your language. But be a blessing to somebody. That's what I think.

—MAYA ANGELOU

The reader will recall from earlier that I had decided to cast away all masks. I found myself in a precarious position whereby inauthenticity was compromising my sense of self and well-being. My unhealthy and unbalanced lifestyle had landed me in the emergency room with severe panic attacks, and it had me rethinking my values, including a reinvestment in hygge culture, interdependence, and Jante's Law. After leaving the hospital and going back to work, I realized that the panic attacks were regular guests in my life and were most often triggered by any episode of *inauthenticity*.

So, I came to the critical and life-changing decision that from then onward, there was going to be only one Robert. I was the same me—to my customers, to my wife, to my colleagues, to my friends, and to myself. It was simply all I could afford. I was ready to lose any of these constituents before I was going to lose myself again. What remained to be discovered was, Who is this Robert? This was the most important lesson I would ever learn, and while it began to close doors immediately, it also started opening others.

Sort of like the Jim Carrey character in the movie *Liar Liar*, I found myself incapable of shape-shifting to meet various client, employee, or executive needs. This is a condition that would simultaneously plague me and serve me even up till the present day. I would like to say that this newfound integrity was helpful when I returned to work, but it had the effect of making things harder for my employer and myself.

This sparked a season of transformation in my life. I began the work of taking off the masks. As a parent, I started to rethink my role with my children; it was more important that they know the real me than the perfect and wise model of an all-knowing parent I had been trying to project. That mask had clearly failed all of us. As a husband, I returned to my wife and her culture more vulnerably. As a leader, I started to draw upon what leaders had modeled in my host culture.

A few years earlier, I had been promoted to a leadership role at Ericsson. With that role came new training courses and mentorships. One of my most valued mentors was a Finnish man named Johan. I had often found many of the Finnish people I met to be somewhat understated and aloof. But Johan did not reflect those qualities! He was a few years older and wiser, very honest, enthusiastic, and plain-spoken in his Finnish accent.

He spoke passionately and joyfully, and everyone seemed to respect his opinions and hang on to his words. In typical Finnish fashion, he was most accessible after a few drinks and perhaps even more so when we were together in the sauna. I loved Johan both as a person and as a leader; he made everyone around him happy and could "challenge" us (his word for negative feedback) but never made us feel unsafe, unvalued, or unheard.

When he promoted me to lead a team of twenty, I immediately had changes in mind. I came to him early with two names of team members I wanted to remove. Johan's advice to me was foreign and unexpected. In his thick accent, he said, "Robert, we do not fire people here; you must fire them up." What he meant, and what I learned, was that we must get to know people as people, not simply as employees. Since it is rather difficult to fire someone (especially seasoned union members) in Scandinavian companies, learning to place them where they would succeed took time and effort.

Along with this wisdom, Johan sent me to Ericsson's leadership training called Leadership Core Curriculum. This is where I learned how to fire people up. It was primarily based on the work of Abraham Maslow. I would learn that understanding the inherent value of other humans and their everyday needs was the key to doing what Johan described; to feed instead of fire people, I needed to know what made them happy. Leadership in this model is less about holding people accountable to the leader's vision than their own self-actualization. In fact, I also learned what made me happy in the process.

Drawing on all of this, I began to look for more answers. I picked up books by Abraham Maslow, and I began to rethink the role of "firing people up." It was in this mindset that I found a book that would change my life. I spotted Tony Hsieh's book at an airport bookstore in Amsterdam.

In *Delivering Happiness*, Tony describes several moments where he chose to be intentional about unfolding his authenticity, including walking away from millions of dollars rather than stay in his agreement with Microsoft after selling Link Exchange, his first large firm. But more important than claiming authenticity, love, and joy as integral to his professional life were what he allowed others as well. It became his whole business plan.

What struck me most about Tony's story was his commitment to his own happiness, stating openly that a rave culture had influenced him and that he longed for the friendship and joy he experienced in his college dorm. I remember thinking, this is what I want from now on—a place where I can be me, bring all of me to work, feel safe and loved, and at end of the day, return home the same way. A place that was hygge, observed Jantes Law, a place to be happy. Had I seen a path back to a position at Ericsson in Norway that had given me most of that, I might still be there today.

> **ENVISION, CREATE, AND BELIEVE IN YOUR OWN UNIVERSE, AND THE UNIVERSE WILL FORM AROUND YOU.**
> **—TONY HSIEH, DELIVERING HAPPINESS: A PATH TO PROFITS, PASSION, AND PURPOSE**

THE MASLOW APPROACH— THREE LEVELS MORE

During this season, I became fascinated by positive and humanistic psychology. Humanistic psychology is a branch of psychology that emerged in the 1950s as a reaction to the dominant psychological approaches of the time, which focused on the study of mental illness and pathology. Humanistic psychology instead focuses on the positive aspects of mental health, well-being, and the unique needs we all share. It is concerned with helping people realize their full potential and achieve self-actualization, which is defined as the ongoing process of actualizing one's potential, capacities, and talents and understanding and accepting one's intrinsic nature. It involves the fulfillment of one's personal mission and an unceasing trend toward unity within oneself. More than about simple sustenance, it could be said that this work is about feeding people what they truly need to be happy and "firing them up."

Abraham Maslow is often considered the founder of humanistic psychology, and his theory of the hierarchy of needs is one of the most well-known contributions to the field. Another major contributor to humanistic psychology is Carl Rogers, who developed the concept of self-theory and the idea of the fully functioning person. According to Rogers, a fully functioning person is one who is open to new experiences, able to make their own decisions, and able to form their own values and beliefs. He believed that the key to mental health and well-being was the ability to be true to oneself and to live in accordance with one's own values and beliefs. Sound familiar yet?

Maslow is well known for his theory of the hierarchy of needs. This theory suggests that people are motivated to meet their needs in order of their importance, with the most basic and urgent needs taking precedence. But many are not aware of the three additional levels Maslow added later.

His first five tiers in the hierarchy of needs are as shown next:

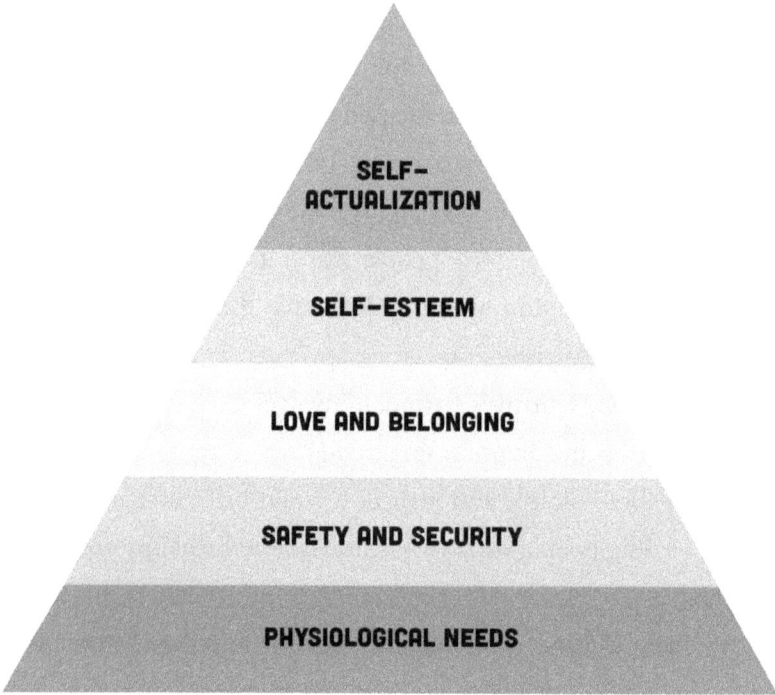

Saul McLeod, "Maslow's hierarchy of needs," illustration, Simply Psychology, last modified January 24, 2024, https://www.simplypsychology.org/maslow.html.

1. *Physiological needs:* These are the most basic and essential needs, such as food, water, shelter, and sleep. When these needs are not being met, nothing else matters.

2. *Safety and security needs:* Once physiological needs are met, the next set of needs to be addressed are those related to safety and security, such as personal security, financial security, and the absence of danger.

3. *Love and belonging:* Once physiological and safety needs are met, people have a desire for love, connection, and a sense of belonging. This includes the need for friendships, romantic relationships, and a sense of community.

4. *Self-esteem:* After love and belonging needs are met, people have a desire for self-esteem and the respect of others. This includes the need for self-respect and the respect of others, as well as achievement and status.

5. *Self-actualization:* Initially, self-actualization was considered the peak of the hierarchy. It is defined as the ongoing process of actualizing one's potential, capacities, and talents and understanding and accepting one's intrinsic nature. It involves the fulfillment of one's personal mission and an unceasing trend toward unity within oneself.

Later, Maslow expanded the hierarchy to include three additional levels:[14]

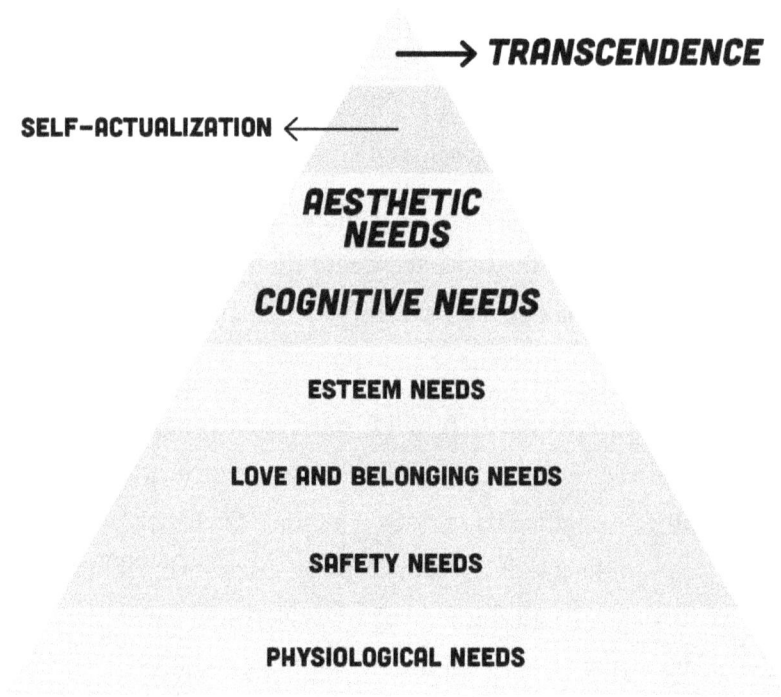

Ibid.

1. *Cognitive needs:* These are needs related to mental stimulation and the desire to learn and explore new things, even if they are not directly related to survival.

2. *Aesthetic needs:* These are needs related to the creation and appreciation of beauty.

3. *Transcendence:* This is the need to go beyond one's own personal interests and concerns and to connect with something larger, such as a higher power, humanitarian causes, or the natural world. This is now considered the highest level of the hierarchy.[15]

By focusing beyond what is wrong with people to what is right with them, Maslow codified what Jante and hygge taught me—that only once we feel that our psychological and safety needs are met can we proceed to the consideration of the third level and topic of this book, which Maslow aptly described as "love and belonging."[16]

When I think of belonging, I remember that my first collective experience was in the Navy. Many shipmates I served with still keep tabs on one another today. Although we have not seen one another for thirty years, I suspect many would come to my aid if I asked them. While most of us suffered in various ways, be it isolation or injury, we yearn for something we lost when we were discharged. In the military, we have a special friendship called *esprit de corps*. It refers to a feeling of pride, fellowship, and common loyalty shared by the members of a particular group.

It is built on shared purpose and sacrifice and from participating in something greater than yourself, putting your safety in the hands of someone in your unit or everyone in your unit. In military jargon, we say, "I've got your six," which refers to the six o'clock position on a clock and means "I've got your back."

The worst sin is to dishonor this intention. For example, in the Marine Corps, when deployed or sharing a meal, senior officers only eat once all their marines are fed. Put another way, even in combat, we keep it hygge.

This is where we enter into a post-egoic, noncompetitive, non-judgmental state, where our ego is secure enough to serve the needs of others ("have their six"), including their esteem and lower-level needs. To share in a hygge moment with others, we must transcend the self and experience non-egoic, abundant, and safe mutual feeding—willful interdependence. We must then set the table with candles, chocolate, and coffee. It is not a competition of who can grab a scarce esteem resource but an egalitarian fellowship that celebrates the abundance we share, when we share. As hard as it is to codify and define, this is hygge in my experience. Once I learned what I was looking for, I found it all around me.

I found that many prominent business books, including from authors like Daniel Pink, Simon Sinek, Patrick Lencioni, and David Logan, were pointing to the same things I had learned abroad: that people need trust, autonomy, mastery, purpose, and transcendence. In addition, I discovered through my own experience in Scandinavia that they need these things collectively once they have them individually. In fact, when they pursue them separately and not as part of an interdependent community, many fall short of human authenticity and fullness. And this is where many Americans I know are confused. We are taught to pursue autonomy and purpose in a ruggedly individualistic fashion, which often is at the expense of others, when it can be argued that perhaps what makes us happy is to share these things with like-minded people. Who among us wants to eat our favorite meal alone?

Shawn Achor is an American positive psychology researcher from Harvard who documented what he called the "Happiness Advantage."[17] This work clearly articulates the connection between happiness and success. It redefined for me the relationship between the two: that we are not happy when we are prosperous but prosperous when we are first happy. In fact, he found that human beings are much more creative, intelligent, and energetic in a state of happiness than when they are sad or neutral. And in case you have not picked up on my message yet, happiness is only in full bloom when it is shared with others in like-minded (hyggelig) collectives, perhaps with candles and coffee.

After traveling to forty-five different countries in search of happiness, Achor discovered that to raise happiness, we need to redefine our equation of happiness, and in return, we will create the outcomes we want. To put this more simply, when we feed people, they thrive; when people thrive, communities thrive. It soon becomes an argument for willful interdependence. If I want to live in a better world, I must gratify the needs of others around me. We must accept that happiness is not over the success horizon. If we wait for happiness only after we succeed and require that others earn our trust and respect, rather than give it freely, we will usually never arrive to the level where we want to be.

In fact, according to Achor, all inputs to success (intelligence, creativity, energy) increase at a state of happiness. Our brains are 31 percent more productive, and it is with our brains that most of us create value.[18] Simply put, the business case for delivering and achieving happiness is willful interdependence.

Marcus Buckingham, an English researcher from Cambridge, has built upon Maslow's principles by researching what makes people happy at work. His work with Gallup in his seminal book, *First, Break All the Rules*,[19] taught us that people are happiest not when they are managed to improve upon weaknesses but when they are allowed to explode their strengths and unfold innate and intrinsic appetites as a part of an authentic collective.

I have read a lot of books about what makes me happy and healthy—not coincidentally, as Maslow tells us, the same things make others happy. I was merging the lessons of Maslow with what I had learned in Scandinavia until I ultimately would discover Laloux's book, *Reinventing Organizations*.[20] This book codified my emerging worldview into something I could explain and was already using to build the company that became Agile Six.

With this simple but profound map, I would learn how to apply hygge to teams and collectives and begin to understand that transcendence is not an individual activity but rather a team sport. To truly be happy in the workplace, we must learn to "feed" one another. To feed one another, we must first understand what we need. The path to happiness, satisfaction, and wholeness at work was willful interdependence—the ability to understand others with empathy, not judgment; to be seen and heard the same way; and to feed and be fed at all levels of Maslow's hierarchy.

> **IF YOU ARE WORKING ON SOMETHING EXCITING THAT YOU REALLY CARE ABOUT, YOU DON'T HAVE TO BE PUSHED. THE VISION PULLS YOU.**
> **—STEVE JOBS**

FINDING MY VISION

Almost exactly one year after picking up Tony Hsieh's book, I was back in the United States looking for a new job. I had three interviews in one week in San Diego, a place my wife and I had always loved. This would be the third time we moved here, and it was never a decision we doubted. I distinctly remember a very rainy winter day a few years earlier in Gothenburg, Sweden, where I was attending a large Ericsson conference.

Perhaps two thousand people in the audience were shown a promotional video for a new transmission product featuring a sail plane flying over a picturesque beach town, idyllic sunny suburbs, golf courses, beaches, and the beautiful Coronado Island in San Diego. I remember wanting to stand up and scream that this was my home. I would keep a copy of that video on my computer desktop for my last few years at Ericsson. It's so easy to see the intersections of fate in one's life when we look back.

Upon my return to the United States, I would interview with three companies, two of which were telecom related. The third was a seemingly random choice, a company that was serving federal clients in support of military family programs. I knew the decision was more serious than previous jobs, and I vowed to be honest, open, and demanding. And I was. I had never been so honest in interviews before. I was leaning toward the third choice, a company called DefenseWeb, because I was looking for more purpose in my work. When I saw the books on shelves around that office, it sealed the deal. Both the hiring manager and the CEO had copies of Tony's book and were passionately able to talk about them. I had found a home, at least for a season.

I was very happy for almost three years at DefenseWeb, which was a direct result of my putting authenticity in the driving seat. I quickly met others who did the same. But as I learned more, I noticed things could and should be done differently. Many among us became growingly aware of better ways to deliver technology and manage teams for the federal government. The books I read led me toward newer, more agile, team-based deliveries, and my responsibilities in the company empowered me to make changes.

So, we did. We implemented Agile Scrum (a methodology in software development that moves control to willfully interdependent teams) transitions and team-building approaches based on another seminal book by David Logan called *Tribal Leadership*. Logan's team had codified much of what I found in Scrum books and *Delivering Happiness*. At the time, it resonated with me as an operating system for self-management. All these pieces would eventually tie together into one place, including the influence of European collective cultures when I came across *Reinventing Organizations*[21] by the Dutchman Fredrick Laloux, as I mentioned earlier.

In this book, Laloux describes most of the epiphanies I have discussed as a component of cultural evolution. He identifies and showcases fifty organizations in the United States and abroad, including Buurtzorg Nederland and Patagonia, who have come to almost all the same weird conclusions as I did. It was inspiring to feel that I was not weird; in fact, I was perhaps evolved. The book describes a model of organizational stages of consciousness, each designated with a color (Red, Amber, Orange, Green, and Teal) to denote progressive evolution toward individual and organizational self-actualization.

TEAL

"TEAL ORGANIZATIONS OPERATE AS LIVING ORGANISMS OR LIVING SYSTEMS. THEY HAVE FOUND THE KEY TO OPERATE EFFECTIVELY WHILE DEALING WITH THE COMPLEXITY OF THEIR ENVIRONMENT. SELF-MANAGEMENT REPLACES HIERARCHICAL PYRAMID. ORGANIZATIONS ARE SEEN AS LIVING ENTITIES, ORIENTED TOWARD REALIZING THEIR POTENTIAL."[22]

GREEN

"GREEN ORGANIZATIONS FOCUS ON CULTURE AND EMPOWERMENT TO ACHIEVE EXTRAORDINARY EMPLOYEE MOTIVATION. THE EMPHASIS ON THE SOFTER ASPECTS OF BUSINESS—VALUES, CULTURE, AND EMPOWERMENT—IS A HEALTHY REACTION TO THE EXCESSES OF ORANGE ORGANIZATIONS."[23]

ORANGE

"ORANGE ORGANIZATIONS STRIVE TO BEAT THE COMPETITION; THE GOAL IS TO ACHIEVE PROFIT AND GROWTH. INNOVATION IS THE KEY TO STAYING AHEAD. MANAGEMENT BY OBJECTIVES, MERITOCRACY, AND ACCOUNTABILITY ARE KEY BREAKTHROUGHS THAT ENABLE ORANGE ORGANIZATIONS TO SCALE."[24]

AMBER

"AMBER ORGANIZATIONS BRING STABILITY AND REPEATABILITY TO RED ORGANIZATIONS. FORMAL ROLES WITHIN A HIERARCHICAL PYRAMID REPLACE THE CONSTANT EXERCISE OF POWER OF RED ORGANIZATIONS. STABILITY IS VALUED ABOVE ALL THROUGH RIGOROUS PROCESSES."[25]

RED

"RED ORGANIZATIONS ARE CHARACTERIZED BY A CONSTANT EXERCISE OF POWER IN INTERPERSONAL RELATIONSHIPS. HIGHLY REACTIVE, RED ORGANIZATIONS CAN RESPOND QUICKLY TO THREATS OR OPPORTUNITIES. THE GLUE THAT HOLDS THEM TOGETHER IS THE PERSONAL BOND TO THE LEADER."[26]

Laloux describes a presently emerging stage as Teal, upon which he presents research and narratives remarkably similar to everything I had learned. Teal cultures as they appear in many communities now strike me as very Scandinavian, focusing heavily on the emergent nature of human beings unfolding in organic collectives to self-actualize in safe and humane companies driven not by dominant and hierarchical leadership models but rather by intrinsic and innate common purposes.

I found Laloux by chance after a season of trying alone to manifest a very similar vision that I thought was a unique expression of my journey. One day, after a few heated and lengthy discussions, a good friend and colleague named Dotti told me, "Robert, you are not seeking self-management; you are looking for Teal."

That day, as I googled the concept, I felt less alone. Laloux details the practices associated with self-management, wholeness, and evolutionary purpose and gives case studies that exemplify said practices. Later in this book, I will share some our practices, most of which have coincidentally been discovered in these other organizations. Laloux saw this pattern and bridged these collectives together under the umbrella of something called Teal.

CHAPTER SEVEN

TRAUMA, HUMILIATION, AND NEURODIVERSITY

He drew a circle that shut me out—
Heretic, rebel, a thing to flout.
But Love and I had the wit to win:
We drew a circle that took him in!

—EDWIN MARKHAM

I am guilty of wasting hours watching TikTok and Meta Reels videos. One of my favorite topics is intragenerational hazing. Gen X (my own people), for example, loves to chastise baby boomers for how we were raised (or neglected) and then brag to millennials and Gen Z that we did not require this supervision. Sometimes, it gets a little darker, and labels like "fragile" or "lazy" get bandied about. In the workplace, it is said that we currently have five generations (traditionalists, baby boomers, Gen X, millennials, and Gen Z). Each generation has something different to offer: more experience on one end and more forward or progressive thinking on the other.

As a Gen X business owner, I sit right in the middle of the field, but as a tech leader, I feel more like the old guy in the room as most of my colleagues tend to be of the millennial or Gen Z type. The changing mindsets of these emerging leaders have sometimes been difficult for me to understand. As a CEO, this has been a source of anxiety but eventually of emotional growth and finally pure opportunity.

These younger folks have known a lot of suffering. They have been bombarded in the media with news of school shootings, pandemic restrictions, and environmental and social justice issues. It's no wonder that many are seeking mental health diagnoses and support more freely than previous generations. They are not fragile though; they are simply demanding resources and safe spaces to survive *and thrive*. Out of necessity and self-awareness, they fix things. I hope that those of us in older generations will abandon the accusations of fragility and instead accept their invitation to deal with our own trauma and build more trauma-aware and trauma-informed workplaces.

A few terms I picked up along the way that are useful for this chapter are as follows.

TRAUMA AWARENESS

Being trauma aware means you have a basic understanding that previous events and adversities can have a lasting impact on individuals. It involves understanding that people may be particularly sensitive to certain stimuli and react in involuntary ways when they are triggered. If you're trauma aware, you recognize that people who have been impacted by trauma need changes to their environment, support, and sometimes therapies and interventions. You may also understand that trauma is prevalent in our society and that the Adverse Childhood Experiences study has shown this prevalence and the connection between early adversities and increased health and mental health risks.[27]

NEURODIVERSITY

Neurodiversity describes the idea that people experience and interact with the world around them in many different ways; there is no one "right" way of thinking, learning, and behaving, and *differences are not viewed as deficits*.[28]

I think a lot about Gen Z, maybe because my son is that age, perhaps because they are just entering our workspaces, or maybe because the media likes to talk about them, often with regard to negative issues like the dangers of social media consumption. A 2022 survey found that 42 percent of them are diagnosed with mental health disorders.[29] According to the American Psychological Association, 27 percent of them say their mental health is fair or poor.[30]

I have heard the narrative that social media is to blame, and I can certainly understand this point; it is hard for me not to feel a little depressed sometimes when overindulging in toxic negative or exaggerated positive social media posts. But cable news is no better.

I think there is something more important and even wonderful going on here. I think they are destigmatizing mental health and the universal human condition of trauma as well as celebrating and *leveraging neurodiversity*. It is this same social media that we blame for injury that they often leverage for success.

As entrepreneurs (and over 75 percent of them aim to be such[31]), Gen Z is celebrating opportunities that neurodiversity brings. A recent ZenBusiness survey found that 92 percent recognized it as a *significant asset*.[32] I believe smart leaders and smart entrepreneurs in older generations will open their hearts and minds to learn from these people who have rejected the social constraints of typical nine-to-five office careers, dominant power structures, and long commutes and shunned them for the gig economy and lucrative enterprises such as content creators, YouTubers, and influencers, expressing their diversity directly to the consumer with insights and interests as unique as the human cognitive spectrum.

When nearly half a generation is diagnosed with mental health challenges and/or neurodivergence, accommodations for this are not simply an exceptional employer policy but rather good business (as is the case for most diversity inclusion policies). They will be a necessity for any firm that wishes to remain viable for any length of time.

Gen Z seems to naturally understand this, as do most millennials, in my experience. In fact, if I am honest, it is my Gen Z and millennial colleagues who have helped me to own my own identity, be grateful for my neurodivergent tendencies, and see the beauty if not utility in my trauma. This has helped me to see past my privilege and place gratitude not in my own abilities but in the people, places, and collectives that have made space for me to thrive. This is the refuge I needed to create the world I needed. I humbly thank Gen Z and welcome them to lead the way.

HUMILIATION

Dr. Evelin Linder is a German Norwegian MD, psychologist, and scholar known for her humiliation theory. The founding president of the Human Dignity and Humiliation Studies and a lecturer at the Centre for Peace Studies of the University of Tromsø, she has committed her life to "engaging with people and communities around the world to ending the cycles of violence resulting from people humiliating or putting other people down."[33]

Typical of many wounded healers, the German native credits her family's traumatic experiences in World War II as foundational to her insights. She is a three-time Nobel Peace Prize nominee. Dr. Linder's work can be considered the complementary perspective of Dr. Rosenberg. Where Rosenberg teaches us how to feed human needs, including dignity, Linder explains how the deprivation of dignity and the subsequent scarcity of esteem is perhaps the source of most human rifts.

She argues "that many of the observable rifts among people may stem from the humiliation that is felt when recognition and respect are lacking … that only if the human desire for respect is cherished, respected, and nurtured, and if people are attributed equal dignity in this process, can differences turn into valuable diversities and sources of enrichment—both globally and locally—instead of sources of disruption."[34]

What we do in response to and to avoid humiliation is perhaps the most prevalent cause of internal, intrapersonal, and global conflict. Often, cycles of violence are proceeded by dehumanization and humiliation. Consider the impact of the following dehumanizing language examples and how these examples serve to pave the way for humiliation and violence:

After the 2016 election, President Donald Trump referred to immigrants as "not people" but "animals."[35]

During the 2016 U.S. presidential election campaign, Democratic nominee Hillary Clinton referred to her opponent's supporters as a "basket of deplorables."[36]

During the Nazi era, the film *The Eternal Jew* depicted Jews as rats.[37]

During the Rwandan genocide, Hutu officials called Tutsis "cockroaches" that needed to be cleared out.[38]

Infliction and avoidance of humiliation are among the most powerful human instincts, which are often referred to as primary emotions.

This cycle (humiliation > dehumanization > violence) is the source of political strife, conflicts, and unhealthy ascensions to power and must be challenged. Perhaps the most widely considered example is the theory that the Treaty of Versailles that ended World War I was the root of World War II. It contained a "war guilt clause" that held the nation of Germany entirely responsible for World War I.

According to the U.S. Holocaust Museum, "The shame of defeat and the 1919 peace settlement played an important role in the rise of Nazism in Germany and the coming of a second 'world war' just twenty years later."[39] This national humiliation was the fuel Hitler used to gin up support for his brutal ambitions. It was revisited on the Jews of Vienna as they were famously forced to clean the streets with a toothbrush.

As I tell the story about my company and colleagues in the following chapters, I have a strong urge to deconstruct much of what has become my public image. Despite my hesitance to accept credit and the humility I picked up in Scandinavia, I sometimes have allowed people to heap praise and gratitude on me. I have occasionally dined in delight on the accolades. I have also read the autobiographies of other entrepreneurs who celebrate their own ingenuity.

Maybe they deserve a victory lap after surviving and thriving through the almost unexplainable level of fear, risk, uncertainty, and hard work that is indicative of entrepreneurship. But I am no superhero, and this is not the tale of my strength or hard work. The things I have done well were born of my weakness, of my trauma, of my neurodivergence, and out of my humiliation.

As I write this, I am nearing the end of my first foray into writing. Oddly, most of the content in this chapter only surfaced in my consciousness once my publishing deadlines drew near. In fact, it was as we approached final line edits, I was reading the autobiography *Surrender*[40] by one of my heroes, Paul David Hewson (a.k.a. Bono, lead singer of the rock band U2), that critical context started falling from the sky. He was telling the story of Iris, the mother he lost at the fragile age of fourteen, the song he wrote about her and how her untimely passing pushed him to become a rock star.

Iris never witnessed Bono's success, and neither did my mom my own. But like Iris, her memory and the trauma of her passing left scars in my psyche. These scars and others were raw and open wounds when we launched the business; collectively, they deserve more credit for the culture we would build than any idea in my head. As I read Bono's account, I realized that I had yet to tell the story of this season, not in this book or even in my own mind. I had to sit down with my wife and reconstruct the timeline of a stormy season beginning in 2014.

I had launched a business, and even as it struggled to find an identity, my nonprofessional world was falling apart. I needed to find refuge, a trauma-aware space where I could feel safe, loved, and heard. It may have been an extraordinary coincidence that I had the power of this new business to build my own refuge. I cannot honestly assert to what degree refuge was by design and what degree by necessity. But this weakened state was the fertile ground upon which we would grow something different. Let me start with when I returned to the United States and my first job at DefenseWeb Technologies.

When I came to DefenseWeb, I was unaware of some critical forces and a season of turmoil that would create professional headwinds for me. As I arrived, the company had been sold to a large healthcare organization called Humana, and the mission would be reshaped during my tenure. Various leaders would rotate within the stumbling company and culture, and none really aligned with my original attraction.

Subsequently, I received mixed reviews. Once, I was told by a CEO in my annual review that I was too "frumpy." "You mean my clothes?" I asked.

"Well, yeah, that too," he said. "You're just frumpy."

I went to HR afterward, not to complain but to ask for a definition of this word. She was somewhat stumped as well. I was simply humiliated.

That year, I got braces, tried to lose a little weight, revamped my wardrobe, and tried to remember to tuck in my shirt and wear matching belt and shoes. To be fair, I think the professional image of many Norwegians is a bit frumpy. It's not unusual to see a law enforcement officer or office worker in a wrinkled shirt or uniform. So maybe it was something I picked up abroad. But honestly, the frumpy me was also frumpy inside. After ten years away, I was different from the sharp and chiseled image of an executive that my leadership wanted. I did not have all the answers, bold plans to execute, or directive orders to shout from my ivory tower. But I could draw on the masks I had picked up abroad. They fit me better. More importantly, I started to take off all masks. I dared instead to be myself and learned to like that guy.

I was asked to help divest the government services division to another company. About a dozen of my colleagues (perhaps half of my division) would follow me directly or indirectly through organizational change as we divested the business to a new employer (Three Wire Systems). When that road ended, I started my own firm, and several of my friends at both firms signed up for that ride. All of us who walked that path together were attracted to the idea of a life without masks. I would like to think they followed the frumpy guy simply because they could see him around the masks.

It was not my intention to start my own firm when I left DefenseWeb but to find a home for my people and for my customers, a place where we could get back to the work of delivering great products for great families. Dan, the founder and CEO of the new firm, was a fellow Veteran with an unquestionable commitment to this mission and his people. He also committed to letting me make it my own, feeding what was, in retrospect, a burgeoning entrepreneurial itch. Dan and I would have some severe disconnects. Eventually, I am sad that we did not sustain a close friendship. But I admire the company he built and how different it was from many in the industry. In the end, it was just not different enough for me.

TRAUMA

Three Wire was a place of temporary refuge for me and my family. In the summer of 2014, my wife, Åse Lill, was diagnosed with triple-negative breast cancer as well as BRCA2, one of two gene mutations known as the breast cancer genes. She had seen doctors about suspicious masses in her breast for years, and it had just become a routine part of our life to get benign results. But to her great credit, she had been diligent with self-exams. The mass had been examined six months prior and determined to be likely harmless but too small to assess appropriately, so the recommendation was a follow-up. This time, the word was malignant, then high-grade, and aggressive.

I am not certain I could handle what she endured that year: aggressive chemotherapy, deep mastectomy, oophorectomy, reconstruction, and more. Still, ten years later, I know she feels incomplete and unwhole. Cancer is a brutal thief, and it often robs us blind, even when we survive. Through the pain and depression, she hardly complained or felt self-pity. She did all this for our family and me, making me want to build the world she deserves to share.

During this challenging season, the leadership and my team at Three Wire taught me a lot about willful interdependence. Many stepped in with gifts, warm cooked meals, and space to step away. Dan and his team passed every test by supporting me without limits. I learned so much from the love that people around us, including our children's classmates, church family, neighbors, and friends, showered upon us. No one let us down. And I always try to pay that forward. As my wife neared the end of her treatments, I decided to launch the company. No longer was I running from toxic workplaces but toward building better places. I had little to lose and all the motivation to be at home with my wife during her extended care. This experience shaped the idea of a remote-first and human-centered business, if not simply so I could work there.

My wife's diagnosis included what is called triple-negative breast cancer, meaning that the tumor was not responsive to the three most usual hormone receptors and, thus, more complicated to treat (fewer options) and more dangerous. We understood that remission risk was higher in the near term and lower after five years. This meant more aggressive treatment and more anxiety in the near term. This made the early years of our entrepreneurial journey more traumatic, and adding to this, I would soon lose the other woman in my life.

The anxiety attacks I had experienced in Norway began to revisit in the spring of 2015. My parents had been in assisted living center, and while Dad was thriving in his ministry, his health was deteriorating. Mom was leaving us a little more every day. We never had a great relationship, and my mother had never been functional in that role. Still, nonetheless, I did love her more than I knew, and to see her waste away at the merciless hands of dementia was more than I could bear, especially as my own wife was still fighting for her life. We visited as often as we could when Åse Lill was strong enough. Looking back, I realize this was the hardest time of my life.

What was I thinking to launch a business with everything else I had on my plate? My Aunt Rose and Uncle Robert were again the rock in my world. I would sometimes call them from the garage or sneak out for a "walk" and wind up in tears. I did not want my wife to see my fear of losing her or my partners to see my fear of failing at the new venture. I had to be strong for everyone. So I started wearing masks again. My father would call me in a panic about little things—Mom had run out of protein shakes, or the nurses had moved his hearing aids. He rarely inquired about my business or my wife's health. He seemed to have all he could handle on his own plate. It frustrated me, and often I would feel anxiety attacks coming on every time his number showed up on my call screen.

I am not sure how much my father really understood about the state of my mom's disease until the very end. We drove the seven hours from our home in San Diego to the dated and underfunded center in the Arizona desert as often as we could manage. Autoimmune diseases had left him recently blind; arthritis had crimpled him, making it impossible to learn braille or walk. In a wheelchair and rapidly losing his hearing, he was fading into a dark place where I could not reach him. Every time I visited, I had to clean his ears, groom his nails, bathe him, and maintain his hearing aids (or try find them in the clutter my mother had collected).

You can imagine my blind father's frustration as Mom would move things around the tiny room they shared, barely a room for two twin beds, a dresser, and a few lawn chairs. She often would forget who he was, much less his disabilities. Recipients of publicly funded care, they were often dirty and underserved. It broke my heart most to have to scream in his ear to explain the details along the path of slowly losing Mom.

Mom's last days were brutal. Anyone who has shared a dementia journey will understand how merciless this condition is. Because mom had developmental challenges her whole life, which already lent themselves to an angry, childlike, and violent disposition, we did not recognize the disease until years into the journey. The diagnosis, about five years late, did give me time to change my own attitude and forgive her. I stopped the judgment and simply took and gave whatever tenderness we could find. And in that season, there were plenty of tender moments. I deeply regret that I had not treated her that way years earlier.

I had seen movies and TV programs depicting Alzheimer's and dementia, and from what I had seen, the patient slowly loses their memories and mental faculties. It looked hard to lose someone this way, perhaps everyone's worst fear. But it's worse than that. In the end stage of these diseases, the brain loses function, not simply memory. Tough decisions must be made, especially if there are no proper advance directives to leverage. I will stop here to ask anyone who reads this to consider sparing this burden for your family and document your preferences, no matter how healthy you are now.

In the last weeks of Mom's journey, her body was not able to swallow food, and she was put on a feeding tube and moved to a more suitable nursing facility for critical care. My father was blind and nearly deaf even when his staff kept proper track of his hearing aids. So, it was almost impossible to discuss the situation, and he sometimes did not understand where she was or when she would return. He often expressed a clueless hope that she was getting better. He had done no research on this condition, or perhaps he had refused to accept the irreversible nature of it. My mom's sisters would visit often. Dad repeatedly asked me to pray for healing; from her sisters, I was reminded that she was a "fighter." But the best and most tragic advice came from a stranger on the phone late one evening.

I answered the phone one evening to hear the voice of what I guessed was an Indian woman on the other end. She had a very covert tone as she apologized for calling so late.

"Are you Cheryl's son?" she asked.

"Yes, I am."

She told me she could lose her job for what she was about to say, but she felt she had to say it.

"Robert," she said, "you need to let your mother go."

At this point, she explained that she was only a product of the healthcare system. She was a source of profit without hope of recovery. She was not coming back, and she was suffering. No one will tell you this because they are not incentivized to do so. The lady never left her name; I would never want to share it. She was part of the healthcare team that was "treating" Mom, and I could hear the sincerity and fear in her voice. The next day, we decided to let Mom go. She was taken off the tubes and sent back to be with Dad in their little room with hospice care for her last few days.

Perhaps I labored through the sad story above to share the better story of those last few days. Because in that story, I found a renewal of my faith and a restoration of my relationship with Mom. Åse Lill was too weak to drive to Arizona to spend the last days with Mom, but my adult daughter and son came along. Last I had seen Mom, she was pale and unconscious, with IVs and tubes to keep her breathing and eating. I read up on hospice care so that I could best support her, my children, and Dad and know what to expect. But as I entered the room, I felt deep relief. I saw her at peace, no tubes or IVs, just resting as if none of this was real. After greeting Dad, the nurse gently woke her up and adjusted her pillows to greet us.

Mom first "embraced" Katherine, looked her dead in the eyes, and smiled. Kat always had a special place in Grandma's heart. In a way, Kat represented not only a granddaughter but also the daughter she lost; she loved Kat perhaps more than anyone in this world. It had bothered me previously, as I felt it neglectful of Kevin, her only grandson, or myself. But now, it just warmed my soul.

But how in hell could Mom be this lucid? For a few hours, she was back! She was in the room with us in a way that she had not been in months or maybe ever. She could not speak, but her eyes and face communicated more than they had in years.

For a few last hours, we all took turns telling her she was loved and seeing tears of joy in her eyes. She had been lost to us for months. She did not know about Åse Lill's battle with cancer, my new business venture, or the struggles Dad was living with, but she knew us. She loved on us without words. Physically, she slipped in and out of sleep. As I had read about, her body systematically redirected resources back to the damaged brain as her extremities started to lose color and fade, toes and hands folding inward. I read that patients sometimes hold on to life longer to let family leave before they go.

So, toward the end, as she fell asleep, I gently whispered in her ear that it was OK to go now and said goodbye. The kids and I gave our final kisses to Dad and Mom and headed home to San Diego. It was only forty-five minutes later on the road when the text came; she was home with her dear lost daughter.

I believe that it is in these times that we see life most clearly. This is not meant to be a religious pitch, but I must share that my mom's passing was the closest I have ever been to absolute faith. I could see my mother's restoration beginning before leaving this world. Her eyes were deep brown again, and I had not seen her smile in months. It felt that she was halfway between worlds, that as she slipped in and out of "sleep," she grew stronger and weaker simultaneously. Mom had a tough life; she dealt with a horrible hand. If anyone deservesd restoration, it was her. Witnessing this, I grew even more convinced that life and, perhaps more so, death are about restoration.

Losing Dad a few years later was no less brutal and without the pleasant goodbye. One had to communicate efficiently with Dad as he was growingly disconnected from the world. I remember praying that he would go home to be with Mom before he lost all contact with this world. In the end, it was a close call. He died of COVID-19 a few years after Mom and a few weeks after an extended battle with pneumonia in a COVID unit. He spent much of his last weeks in isolation, his hearing aids lost by neglect, and as was the protocol at that time, he was unable to receive visitors. I would ask the nurse to hold the phone to his ears while I tried to scream into the receiver that he was loved and that we were there. Some days, he could speak back; others, he could only make labored guttural groans.

Dad left us his own spiritual message. I like to call it his last sermon. After he beat pneumonia, we decided to send him back to the center, to the room where he and Mom had lived and Mom had passed on, for his own hospice care. It was generally expected that he was in his last months. He had spent about a month in the COVID unit. We did have a few conversations, and he shared a precious last message with me.

Dad had experienced a near-death experience in the throes of the pneumonia; he believed he had walked and talked many hours with his savior in heaven. I never got to see him face-to-face again, but he would recount to others, including his sister, Rose, and other family members much of what Jesus told him. Fortunately, they recorded it for me, and I have watched it many times.

While the details were hard to gather, he had been given a message very much like this book! In his own words, Dad spoke of seeing people and embracing trauma as the source of real shared experiences. The following is a direct quote, and among the last words I have from Pastor Jim:

We all want to rush past the bad times, but the real friendships, the real memories that you have when you look back, are more likely to have come from one of those bad times ... you can't rush through bad times to get the good times ... life is a journey. The bad times happen from the day you're born until the journey is over ... It's how you live the journey that brings meaning to your life, not getting to the end, because when you get to the end, you probably won't like it.

With the short time we have in this world, we are all here to feed and restore one another, and so I got back to work to build a business with these significant lessons at the forefront.

How do we reinvent organizations so that people are authentically heard? How do we leverage their diversity? How do we create trauma-informed communities where real humans are safe to unfold love into what they're doing and each other?

That ambition has motivated me ever since. I know that life is not always sunshine and lollipops. In fact, we learn more and unfold more when it is not.

Still, an employer can add to the wholeness of its employees. My goal was to create an environment where people could bring their authentic selves to work, stay home when unwell, and respect the wholeness of others. Together, we built an environment of wholeness, trust, and inclusion. I learned this in Norway and then from my Gen Z and millennial colleagues.

By owning my fear of humiliation, embracing diversity, and breaking the stigma and cycle of trauma, beauty can emerge. As they ascend to leadership, or start their own firms, millennials and Gen Z are demanding and building the collectives we all need, emphasizing the importance of creating a refuge where people can be vulnerable and heal together.

They are not fragile; they are equipped. Fragility is leaving trauma and diversity buried, thinking it's in the past when in fact it's holding us back. As I start to tell more of my story, please see their contribution.

In the pages that follow, I will share the successes I have experienced through the journey of building Agile Six. However, I cannot take credit for anything more than being in a broken place, being ready to listen to people different from myself, be they of different cultures, identities, or generations. They gave me what I needed and helped me build something closer to what the future will simply demand.

CHAPTER EIGHT

ANSWERING THE CALL

---

*If you want to build a ship, don't drum up the men
to gather wood, divide the work, and give orders.
Instead, teach them to yearn for the vast and endless
sea.*

—ANTOINE DE SAINT-EXUPÉRY

Sometimes when speaking to people about the government contracting business (or "GovCon" for insiders), I describe it like a concrete wall you must claw through with your bare hands. It's not an easy business to break into, but once inside, the wall tends to make you feel safe and sheltered. On my birthday in 2014, my cousin Ernie and I decided to get some cinder block under our fingernails. In retrospect, it was a remarkably casual discussion that ended in a decision to change the world. The conversation started with a birthday text from Ernie. It escalated somehow to a kind of marriage proposal. "Hey, how about we risk our family's life savings together?"

Ernie showed up in my life when I was about five years old, and he was less than a year younger. As you will recall, my home life at that point was lacking. Ernie would become a best friend and my rock until I met my wife. His early childhood had also left him vulnerable, and we honestly and immediately had each other's back. He and his darling baby sister, Sherry, quickly became like siblings to me, and as I mentioned earlier, his mother, Rose, was my second mother. On Christmas mornings, our first calls were to each other to share the joy of our bounty. It's much like that today—the good news is only as good once I share it with him.

I have had some time to share my manuscript with Ernie before finalizing it for this book. We talked about our childhood and the recollections we have of our challenges. Ernie was not the first person to tell me that I was a bully to him at times. The Jackal is indeed a sneaky bastard. I reassured Ernie, and I do now to the world, that I had no violent intentions myself. It helps me have empathy for those who bullied me at times.

As Rosenberg tells us, everything we do is in service of our needs. When this concept is applied to our view of others, we'll see that we have no real enemies, that what others do to us is the best possible thing they know to do to get their needs met.[41] I feel that most of the time now, Ernie and I feed each other's needs and ask for clarification when judgment is perceived. This is a skill that I would love to have had in my pocket back then.

As children, we had a few ventures together: we shared a baseball card collection, a candy-vending business, and many schemes of less venerable qualities. As transient as our family was, he became a rare, ongoing, and healthy attachment for me. Unsurprisingly, I wanted to have him closer and share a business throughout my life. Unlike myself, Ernie had buckled down and been a successful student, earned a reputable business degree, founded a company, and sold it to Amazon. So, he brought the early muscle in a business sense. He set up all the details I found mundane but made us professional.

To this day, he is the very best chief financial officer that I know. Our firm never had to borrow money, never risked missing payroll, and never had to factor (borrow against) our invoices. And to his great credit and my most amazing gratitude, he was willing to follow undereducated, unproven me. Despite his qualifications and skills, I have often wondered if I could have mustered the humility and grace to follow him. For me, following was always more complicated than leading.

When I got off the phone on my birthday, I made a list of words I was feeling, words that reflected what I wanted for my government, for my home life and for my company, words like "trust," "agility," "comradery," "humanity," and so on. The next step involved a few hours of domain searching and name searches on the California Secretary of State's website. One critical decision factor in our name was that all significant domains of Agile6.xxx were available.

So, what does the name mean? After confessing to a practical start to our name search, I will still try to convince you that it has deep meaning. It really does. First, the word is "agile." The Agile Manifesto always has and still speaks to me deeply. More than a methodology of building products around users and delivering constant value, it is also a recipe for better government and less toxic politics:

> *WE ARE UNCOVERING BETTER WAYS OF DEVELOPING SOFTWARE BY DOING IT AND HELPING OTHERS DO IT. THROUGH THIS WORK, WE HAVE COME TO VALUE:*
>
> - *INDIVIDUALS AND INTERACTIONS OVER PROCESSES AND TOOLS*
> - *WORKING SOFTWARE OVER COMPREHENSIVE DOCUMENTATION*
> - *CUSTOMER COLLABORATION OVER CONTRACT NEGOTIATION*
> - *RESPONDING TO CHANGE OVER FOLLOWING A PLAN*
>
> *THAT IS, WHILE THERE IS VALUE IN THE ITEMS ON THE RIGHT, WE VALUE THE ITEMS ON THE LEFT MORE.*

We believed that referencing this manifesto would animate our staff to unfold more autonomously around the products and people we serve and leave the process to a minimum. For an agile software company, this choice seems easy enough. But what about the "six"? This may take more explanation. The most straightforward answer is that we have an expression, "I've got your six," in the military. This is a promise that a teammate has your back, or on a clock, your six o'clock position.

In military jargon, it means, "Trust me, take the risk; I am on your side, and no one is going to hurt you where you are most vulnerable if I am here." In our world at Agile Six, this means we can be authentic, vulnerable, and safe; we can unfold more deeply and reveal our true selves because we know our teammates have our backs.

That answer is nearly sufficient. It describes the culture I wanted for myself, my partners, and my colleagues. It also is a promise to our clients and country that if you put your trust in us, we will have your six. This is not a guarantee of success; we may make mistakes or fall down, but we will do so while fighting earnestly and for your interests and our shared mission to improve our government. But there was something more to this part of the name. It is also a call to all Americans to do more of the same for one another.

I have mentioned briefly that I was a child of poverty. I have known the problematic experiences of digging in trash cans for food and sleeping in unsafe or unsheltered places. For me and countless other young people who enlisted, the military is the first place that truly had our six. It is perhaps the most effective program for millions of Americans to climb out of poverty and social strife. In boot camp, I had my first dental work, and my first formal wardrobe was navy blue!

I am often thanked for my service, and it honestly feels awkward. It is I who should be thankful. Despite only occasionally liking the actual work of being a sailor, I have no idea where I would be today without the Navy. If I can ask for anything in return for my service, it is that, as a nation, we find better opportunities to support and escalate vulnerable people than warfighting.

So, in late 2014, Ernie and I launched our crazy idea of starting a company. Ernie focused on the mechanics of the business, and I built a vision and team. I had rehearsed much of this in my mind for months. I would call the most brilliant people I knew and hope a few would sign up. I expected to make many phone calls; after all, we needed a lot of competence. So, I was surprised and elated when my two first calls were successful.

Brian Derfer was my colleague at DefenseWeb and my first thought after Ernie. Besides being a brilliant technical thinker, I have always encountered him as the most sincere and honest broker I know. He will admit and remedy something if he does not understand it. The second call was to Edward Teeple, someone I had known since my time in the Navy. Edward had stayed in the defense cybersecurity community. He brought a critical ability to secure the solutions that Brian would design. But like Brian and Ernie, his unsurpassed integrity and generosity attracted me the most. With that, our founder's team was set. The next step was to figure out what we could offer the world together.

The four founders locked themselves in a cabin in Lake Arrowhead, California, for three days to collaborate on our business plan. None of us were younger than forty, we were all parents, and we had diverse professional backgrounds. The idea was to put all our strengths in a pile and examine them. But we spent the most time discussing our values and aligning our passions. In retrospect, this was the most crucial discussion we would ever have.

Compared with most start-ups, we were less egoic, not necessarily wanting to prove something to the world but with more desire to improve it. Our values would evolve later as our company grew in size and diversity, but what we came up with initially were integrity, commitment, initiative, and fun.

As I recall, the commitment to integrity was my strongest ask (given my previous bout with an identity crisis). It took a long time to persuade the others. It was not that they did not believe in integrity, but they did not want to include it lightly. We were all too tired of companies saying this and not delivering. I often explain to my colleagues that integrity resonated for me from my Navy days. Onboard the USS *Kitty Hawk*, we had all kinds of people, pilots, mechanics, lawyers, doctors, cooks, and so on.

But whenever there was an integrity issue with the ship, be it fire on the flight deck or a rupture in the hull, we were all trained as firefighters and/or damage controllers. And regardless of our reason for being on the ship, the integrity of the ship came first. The famous last words of James Lawrence captain of the USS *Chesapeake* during the war of 1812 are well known in naval circles: "Don't give up the ship."[42] It is the battle cry of the U.S. Naval Academy and the theme of a 1935 film *Shipmates Forever*.

Over the years, this value evolved for me as it became a reflection of not only what I expected of myself (personal integrity) but also what I needed from others (authenticity) and in collectives into the word "wholeness," and even today, no word is more important in our culture. It is a challenge to every member of our staff (whom we refer to internally as Sixers) to speak up with courage and honesty, challenge one another (including me), and point out any lapse or even perceived lapse in the integrity of our ship. I often say, for the sake of all aboard, point out the holes in the boat; don't walk by them.

I recall after setting and committing to our values, we focused on what we could contribute to the world. We all felt that our careers had been somewhat meaningless. Yes, we had done well feeding our families and developing ourselves and others. Still, the products we had each developed were mainly about entertaining and connecting people. We decided we wanted to do something big. We wanted to improve our government. I recall Brian and Ernie, in particular, feeling called to start with Veterans because they had not served in the military.

So, on a whiteboard, we drew a circle around the word "VA" (Veterans Administration); then in a concentric circle, every organization, person, or firm we knew who was in any way connected to the VA; and then finally, in another circle, everyone we knew with first- or second-degree connections to those people. We had our targets. After assessing our skills, we decided to start with human-centered software development. A short time later, we developed our "just cause," which was admittedly complicated, that of "restoring human-centered agency in our governments, communities and workplace." It would eventually evolve into what it is today: "We build better by putting people first."

PUTTING PEOPLE FIRST

During my time in Norway, I resonated deeply with professional environments that prioritized humanistic autonomy—where trust is given freely rather than earned—and value egalitarian, flat structures. This perspective aligns with the Teal movement's self-management philosophy, as Frederic Laloux elaborated in *Reinventing Organizations*. At its core, it's about recognizing that individuals know their life contexts and values better than any manager ever could.

If we truly believe in people's innate trustworthiness and motivation, then we must provide them the space to dictate more of their own terms. This means understanding that only individuals can grasp their current personal and family dynamics. A manager can't and shouldn't attempt to do so. If we're aligned in our mission, we must trust people and step aside. If doubts arise about someone's integrity, if you think they will poke holes in the ship, it's better to separate from them or if possible, not to bring them on board. They will after all live and professionally die on our ship.

I envision this trust-based relationship as the bedrock of employment. It's about mutual growth and authenticity. I often tell my team our goal isn't to be the "best place to work" but to create the most genuine work environment. We may not have an office with lounge space or the most generous benefits out there, but our company is a sanctuary for those who seek authenticity over accolades, a place to be true to oneself. My aim isn't to claim superiority in this approach but to attract like-minded individuals who prioritize living authentically over merely working. There's a need for spaces that champion this philosophy.

CHALLENGES AND REWARDS OF AN EQUITABLE WORK ENVIRONMENT

So naturally, Agile Six is primarily a flat structure. Today, even as we grow past one hundred employees, we operate with a handful of executives, peer coaches, and zero managers. I recently communicated to our coaches that while our environment is nurturing and safe, it may not resonate with everyone. We've consciously designed a non-competitive and egalitarian workspace, where one's intrinsic value matters more than climbing traditional career ladders. While there's potential for profound career journeys here, we don't cater to conventional definitions of "career development." Such traditional career paths have their place, and I acknowledge their importance to many individuals. Yet, there's a burgeoning realization about happiness through wholeness and self-management among many Americans who now seek meaningful work beyond status and titles. Gen Z, in particular, does not want to wait fifteen years in order to have a voice in the world. Case in point: a recent job posting of ours attracted over 1,800 applicants in just a few days.

Our organization thrives on equity and collaboration, offering equal pay for equal work within a nonhierarchical structure. This setup may feel unstimulating for those conditioned to chase promotions and seek uneven advantages. I recall stepping out of a comfortable European job, driven by ambition and desire for more challenging roles. Though it led me to extreme stress and eventually sparked the creation of our company, it remains a pivotal juncture in my journey.

Many top-tier talents, nurtured in cutthroat environments, yearn for challenges that push their limits. I felt the same in Norway. Our focus has since been on integrating fresh initiatives and resources to ensure that even purposeful work stays varied. Like all sectors, our business has its highs and lows. During quieter periods, rather than perpetuating fear of idle times, we believe in empowering our team to manage their work schedules and make the most of these phases. Go home.

Instead of the common practice of hiring during peaks and cutting staff during slumps for "efficiency," we prioritize trust and continuity. Excessive layoffs lead to a distrustful atmosphere, and a fear of downtime can drive employees away. We aim for a balance, ensuring our team can take a step back when needed without fear of repercussions. We do end up in circumstances where employees are idle and have no apparent road map to a new project or function. In this case, we still endeavor to have their six, even if it means parting ways as compassionately as possible. But we do not look for redundancy simply as a routine method to balance our costs.

The absence of managerial overhead often results in the very efficiency we crave. Ironically, humans often inadvertently manufacture the scarcity they're trying to avoid. But when we trust, discard the scarcity mindset, and foster abundance, we invariably witness it. Empowered and self-reliant employees navigate work cycles organically, fostering innovation and unveiling new horizons. After all, according to Achor, happy individuals are 31 percent more creative.[43]

Foregoing traditional management means fewer corporate ladders and fewer external motivations for "extra efforts" or "special initiatives." While many initially relish stepping off the corporate treadmill, adjusting can be akin to retirees facing an identity void. I argue it's beneficial to face this realization early, questioning the blind ambition that propels many from school to retirement without reflecting on personal purpose.

Our competitive society instills this relentless race from a tender age. I reject most forms of professional competition; employees within a company should not be pitted against one another in competition for resources. I would much rather our collective contend with big problems, such as poor healthcare or inaccessible government. At our company, we won't fabricate hierarchies or career trajectories to dangle challenges or rewards, and no one receives a merit bonus or performance-based pay raise. My perspective deviates from the norm, and here's my take from a recent discussion in a chat room with our coaches:

Team, one of the cultural differences I have witnessed with European flat structures (which are closer to Teal) is that people "work to live" and do not "live to work." One of my intentions with Agile Six was to welcome people like myself. It's a place where you can (for long seasons or short) enjoy balance, do your job with pride and kindness, and go home on time or early if nothing is pressing. I suspect this gets boring sometimes, some of the boredom is unexpressed agency or energy that might be better placed outside of our walls, and that is MORE than OK; that needs to be embraced.

For others and other seasons, extracurricular improvement initiatives are a great outlet as may be more challenging roles if they emerge organically. I just don't want to push them as THE answer to boredom.

Boredom is a personal issue. And no one should feel that there is political gain or loss from extra initiative. We removed the word "initiative" from our core values some time ago; for this reason, it's not bad, but it does not all need to be spent here at work.

The insights I've shared might be met with skepticism. It has taken years of nurturing trust and understanding within my team for these beliefs to truly resonate with them. Yet, I am profoundly convinced of their validity. Consider what is possible if you embrace these concepts with an open heart and test them yourself over time.

1. The product of teams with less individualistic ambition and more collective ambitions does not suffer. The heuristic product of creative, happy, balanced, and inspired people in less competitive teams will outperform those built hastily in politically unsafe spaces.

2. Whole people who are outstanding in their community, have time for their families, serve other interests (e.g., part-time musicians, athletes, and artists), take vacations, and seek inspiration in the wider world create great products, sustainably, in less time.

3. In the traditional hierarchical structures I have witnessed, I believe up to 60 percent of time and energy is spent on political maneuvering and competing for artificially scarce resources like proximity to power. How many needless meetings are filled with useless discourse meant primarily to position for advancement or ease the mind of a distrustful manager? This negative energy is nonregenerative, meaning it creates more scarcity in our creative minds and in our day as we ruminate over political slights and missed opportunities.

ENTREPRENEURSHIP

Ernie and I set our lives up around the idea that we would go two years without a paycheck (which was very close to the case). Ernie, having succeeded in a previous venture, was the most financially prepared. However, he was betting this hard-earned small fortune on us. For my part, I sold our 401(k)s, took a mortgage on our home, and requested limit increases on all our credit cards before leaving my job. Brian and Edward would receive basic salaries, but they would also be the billable product. I was incredibly humbled by the sacrifices everyone made, working long days in low-paid or unpaid roles, where they were all overqualified, and then long nights writing proposals and hoping to grow our company, improve our work, or hopefully both.

Inside the brick wall of government contracting was another brick wall that existed around the niche of a bourgeoning new sector we call Civic Tech. They played by different rules than the community at large. One could pick up several books and get advice about "selling to the government" or "working with con-tracting officers," but those rules were being rapidly rewritten (for the better) by two federal agencies: U.S. Digital Service (USDS) and the General Services Administration unit called 18F (so named for their location at the corner of Eighteenth and F streets in DC). These people, many of whom were nontraditional federal employees, came from places like Google and brought innovation and agility to the government. Within the "GovCon" industry, this formed a disruptive movement called Civic Tech, something we will discuss in the next chapters.

To their great credit, they made it a regular habit to pierce the walls and go out looking for talent and companies from the private sector. Had we been an existing technology company with a good track record, we could have leveraged this community to skip paying our dues in the more significant federal contracting space. But we had yet to have any past performance. So, our mission was to pierce both brick walls with little to offer except our personal résumés, passions, and ideas.

I had contacts in the industry at large, so the plan was twofold: first, reach out to those people we knew in GovCon, start paying our dues (which meant performing any menial work we could get, as well as long nights of proposal writing), and, at the same time, seek new relationships with people who could give us the work we wanted (which would mean traveling the country stalking these young Civic Tech leaders at any conference or presentation they offered). The plan was that the former would keep the lights on while we developed the ladder. And it worked to a large degree.

As inexperienced as we were as a brand, we had to visit many Beltway companies hat in hand and basically ask for table scraps. We would put in long hours writing proposals for them, often for work where they had no priority because of the low probability of winning, and then promise them the bulk of any margins while we worked for low wages. One thing we did have was the military experience of Edward and me. As we had suffered injuries while enlisted, we were certified by the VA as a Service Disabled, Veteran-Owned Small Business (SDVOSB).

Under this program, there are goals for both government buyers and federal contractors to hire us. So, our original proposition was to be the most talented SDVOSB, if not the least experienced.

The immediate outcome was that we managed to get teaming relationships (subcontractor roles) on nineteen losing bid teams in the first two years. It felt futile as these nineteen proposals took up so much of our time and ultimately yielded no revenue. It would not be an exaggeration to say that after the first two years, we were disheartened, exhausted, and bleeding financially. I have heard that the most crucial factor in a start-up is not capabilities, funding, or imagination but simply the density of determination. This was our secret weapon! At least on my end, I had burned through every ounce of savings and equity in my home before we won our first deal. Fortunately, I never had to start using credit cards to pay my bills, but I would have.

I remember telling the team, I am in this forever. There is no plan B. We were all highly qualified, and we could have taken a job outside the company at any time. We usually managed to keep Brian and Edward busy doing mediocre work during the day and writing modest proposals at night. Ernie had kept us cash-positive the whole time. Ernie and I would travel to conventions to drum up business even as we shared hotel rooms to limit the costs. I remember telling the team to just put a car on the road (get some revenue), and we would manage to turn it when we had momentum (do better work).

I met Dan Levenson at a typical conference in downtown Washington, DC, in the winter of 2016. Dan was a contracting officer (government speak for a buyer) at the Centers for Medicare and Medicaid Services (CMS). He was in the eye of a storm (I will discuss the Healthcare.gov website crash in the coming chapters) that would generate much of the inertia needed to create the Civic Tech movement and had developed a reputation and relationships with the key people I was trying to reach.

Dan's passion and gift was for reinventing the contracting approaches of government to work with the traditional but cumbersome regulations (known as the federal acquisition regulations) in an approach that would come to be known as objective-based contracting. I never knew there could be so much innovation in acquisition. Still, there was, and Dan was brilliantly reshaping the relationship of his agency to break through the brick walls I mentioned to attract more talent to the technical problems and hold industry more accountable. Dan was a part of a growing group of contracting officers (federal buyers) that were calling themselves "bureaucracy hackers," intentionally sticking fingers into the sausage machine.

So, when I heard that he was on a panel in DC, I flew across the country hoping to get my business card in his hands. Toward the end of the panel discussion, where hundreds of industry professionals (mostly more traditional) had come to hear him and others, I stood up with a question for Dan that would change our fate. My question that I had meticulously prepared and nervously delivered struck a nerve and was from my own experience with Agile in previous firms. "Mr. Levenson," I started (with much anxiety), "do you really think the government can own its own products?"

Product ownership in Agile software teams is the role of understanding the users; it's the barista of the "warm cup of coffee." It takes an understanding of a digital product's capabilities, consumer needs, team dynamics (although here, there is another supporting role called a Scrum Master), and available resources. The catch-22 is that, as the name would indicate, ownership is something difficult to outsource. So often, federal employees with limited training, experience, or intuition in this role would be charged to set priorities for development teams staffed by contractors.

This relationship was strained further by commercial interests, especially when requirements were vague, and compensation was by the hour. Objective-based contracting would evolve to fix the ladder problem (hourly compensation replaced by outcome-based incentives), and we set ourselves up to improve the former (educate federal product owners). Product ownership was something we knew very well from our private sector careers. So, long story short, we won our first subcontract working for CMS, teaching Agile Scrum and, in particular, product ownership to stakeholders at CMS.

CMS was headquartered in Baltimore, and we were too cash-strapped to hire local staff. We also wanted to keep our first promises personally. So, Ernie would commute, and I would temporarily move from California to Baltimore to deliver this first official contract. We would both be Agile coaches and work very closely with Dan Levenson and the folks at USDS. This afforded us so many learning and networking opportunities.

While it "conflicted" us out of many deals (a term that meant we knew too much internally to compete for larger software development work), we were working behind the scenes with our future buyers, helping them to select, hire, and work with people like us. In the following year, we won our first prime contracts (meaning working directly for the government and not through a subcontract to another firm) doing the same and became known at CMS as an Agile and acquisition coaching shop. It was a vital lesson in existential flexibility. We did not set out to be an Agile coaching shop, but we found someone with a need we could fill. And then we went all in on that need.

Interestingly, even as our reputation as honest brokers and trusted partners for coaching at CMS started to develop, we also began making inroads as an engineering shop at the VA.

This empowered Brian and Edward to walk away from some of the less desirable work that kept the bills paid and focus on being more authentic to our own passions. After about three years, we had our "car on the road" and could start turning it in our desired direction. Incidentally, everyone was drawing a meager salary, making the future feel infinitely more viable.

Today, I have the occasional opportunity to mentor new Veteran entrepreneurs. I can very quickly spot those who will succeed.

It comes down to a few things, and I would only suggest this path if you have them.

First and foremost, a good "why." What in the world do you want to fix?

1. What is your why, and what is alive in you? The more authentic this answer is, the easier the second one will be.

2. Next, you must be stubborn as hell. Nothing replaces density of determination. Are you ready to sleep in cheap hotel rooms nationwide while going into debt at home, all in service of your "why"?

3. Existential flexibility is the ability to sense and respond to what you hear when you meet potential clients. You need to be able to understand what you have that they genuinely need and lean into that. This one is hard because you must maintain authenticity, or you can get lost quickly. This means seeing your "why" even during detours.

4. You must have the ability to attract people more intelligent than yourself. Ultimately, the bet is on other people. The sooner you realize that your role is to build their dreams in service of yours, the better. What is alive in them? Remember that you must feed those intrinsic motives in others. This will inform and evolve your "why" into a collective "our why." Carrots and sticks lead to transactional relationships, and transactional relationships will always eventually fail.

I found all this in my relationship with my first client. Dan Levenson and I quickly formed a bond through our work that would transform the company. His integrity and ingenuity surpassed my expectations, but his trust in me was the currency I needed. After spending almost three years writing traditional dry proposals, chasing after almost mythical USDS personalities, and pleading with my team for resilience, we were finally working with a client and making the world better.

Dan and his colleagues at CMS trusted us to work one on one with federal employees, to coach critical teams on delivery matters, and to teach courses on topics such as scrum, leadership, product management, and even, eventually, objective-based acquisition. I grew incredibly fond of the employees at CMS. Despite the season when the agency was somewhat under political discourse, and despite the cruel stereotypes of lazy federal employees and "deep state" accusations, I met people who came to the government to help others. I can recall at least a few literally crying in one-on-one meetings where they started to see new opportunities to recognize the agency they sought when joining the federal service. I saw passion, I saw hard work, I saw resilience, and I saw outcomes.

It was during this time that I began to see the fruits of our collective labor. Projects that we coached not only achieved their goals but also became benchmarks for efficiency and effectiveness within the agency. Incidentally, this role put us in the trenches with the Civic Tech icons from the USDS we had been stalking. Courses we taught inspired innovations in process management, leading to more agile and responsive delivery of services to the public. Each breakthrough in collaboration and each success story were testaments to the potential within these teams—an affirmation of what can be achieved with commitment and hard work.

As I reflect on those powerful moments—moments of genuine emotion from employees who saw new possibilities for the agency they cherished—I am reminded of the strength that lies in resilience and unity. These experiences have reinforced my belief in the power of collective effort and have shaped my resolve to further this impact beyond the confines of any single institution.

To the skeptics who doubt the integrity and value of federal workers, I extend an invitation to witness the dedication firsthand by stepping into these roles. It is my promise to you that the experience will be far more demanding and rewarding than you could imagine.

Now, as I stand at the threshold of a new chapter, I carry with me the lessons and insights from CMS, ready to sow the seeds of transformation on a broader scale. The journey at CMS was just the beginning, a prologue to a larger story of change and innovation that I am eager to write. What lies ahead is a path uncharted, filled with opportunities to leverage my experiences and ignite a greater impact. Stay tuned for what's to come—the best is yet to unfold.

CHAPTER NINE

MAKING SAUSAGE

---

*A political party—it's like a sausage grinder; it grinds
all the heads up together into one mash, and then
it turns them out, link by link, into fatheads and
meatheads! The struggle for liberty is nothing but the
constant active appropriation of the idea of liberty.*

—HENRIK IBSEN, *AN ENEMY OF THE PEOPLE*

In the previous chapters, I told you much about how my life has informed my leadership approach. It has also influenced the place where I chose to work. It was my pursuit of purpose after my existential crisis in Europe that brought me into this federal contracting space, and that is why Agile Six continues to seek its purpose here. I have spent most of my career in the proximity of federal technology projects, the most prominent exception being my ten years in Europe. I believe strongly that this sector has a sacred obligation to steward the collective resources of the nation and to reduce the friction caused by taxation and governance with better customer experiences. Also, and to be very open, I felt it was a great place to experiment with the management ideas I wanted to apply.

Far from the front lines of commercial product development, where cutthroat executives race to capture new markets, federal contracting is stable and packed with intrinsic purpose. I also had a suspicion that a lot could be achieved toward healing the discord of the American culture wars by creating a government that everyone believed in. To this end, I could deliver on what would later become known as reflected in our tagline "Better place to work. Better work to do." But before I can brag about what we have achieved in this space, I must take some time to explain where it is and where we meet our clients.

The federal government's constitutional purpose is "to establish Justice, ensure domestic Tranquility, provide for the common Defense, promote the general Welfare, and secure the Blessings of Liberty to ourselves and our Posterity."[44] Ideally, government spending achieves these goals.

To bring back the analogy used in the beginning of this book, the federal government is a large boat with two-and-a-half centuries of tangled lines underneath it. If any organization, with any mission of any size, had those many tangles, it would have been abandoned long ago. Millions of amazing people working within this ecosystem are making furious and sometimes futile attempts to untie these knots. But the structures are such that many of those in authority elected by the people auspiciously to administer the constitutional purpose above have abandoned it altogether. Words like "tranquility," "general welfare," "blessings of liberty," and "posterity" are rare around the capital, and it's no wonder that Congress has the lowest approval rating in recent history. It is nothing if not violent, and it repels or destroys all who approach it with a spirit of nonviolence.

I often tell new employees in our firm to be very patient and expect fear-based ecosystems and the gridlock they induce in government. Still, I also remind them that the U.S. government is the single most funded and potentially effective agent for change in the history of the world. I ask them to get up every morning and bump it. If we bump it, even a little daily, we can change the world. I wish those we elect and empower to bump it harder would embrace NVC, willful interdependence, and abundance.

Much has been written about the experience of expatriation. Mark Twain said, "Travel is fatal to prejudice, bigotry, and narrow-mindedness."[45] It is among the most important things I have ever done to experience the world from outside my home country, and I recommend it to everyone. Having met many expatriates (expats), I am familiar with the cycle that begins with a honeymoon phase, where the host country is fresh and new; everything is better than home. This is followed eventually by a time of frustration where, oddly, nothing is as good as home, and all ideas contrary to our upbringing are just wrong. The third phase includes empathy development for the nuanced differences where the expat begins to tolerate and understand cultural nuance. The final phase is ownership. This is where I arrived in Scandinavia.

Over time, my perspectives have shifted. I have witnessed and felt the benefits and advantages of less violent, more collective approaches to politics, culture, and governance. I began to appreciate the value of a society prioritizing collective well-being, enabling its citizens, particularly children, to focus on realizing their true potential. Ensuring everyone's basic needs are met allows individuals to evolve, pursue their passions, and grow without being constantly burdened by existential fears. In my opinion, this is a constitutional role of the government described as to "secure the Blessings of Liberty to ourselves and our Posterity."[46]

When I returned to the United States, I knew politics and culture had become extreme battlegrounds, and I had perhaps switched sides or at least moved to the left. But I must say that I did not expect this to emerge to the degree it did in the wake of the Obama administration. It was truly shocking and heartbreaking to witness Americans' divided nature. Perhaps as a result, I sensed the contrast between the experience that the Norwegian government had given me and what the U.S. federal government was giving its citizens.

For example, the tax authority in Norway had for many years eliminated most of the burden of tax preparation. Norwegians have had safe digital identities across all federal services for at least twenty years. So, not only is citizen data secure in the hands of the government, but it is accessible to their daily life. So, when it is time to settle your taxes in Norway, you electronically receive a simple reconciled statement from the authorities. Suppose one agrees (and 95 percent of the time we have) that the simple information and calculations are correct. In that case, one approves it using their government-supplied pin codes, and it is done in five minutes or less. Even more impressively, this same universal ID is used across all federal agencies, so if I need to check the status of my pension payment, stop my mail, or even schedule a doctor's appointment, it is the same.

Setting aside the topics of lobbyists and various special interest groups (a decision that will keep me within my word count), our two-party system has evolved toward violent conflict rather than compromise.

Consider the words of George Washington from his Farewell Address in 1796:[47]

> THERE IS AN OPINION THAT PARTIES IN FREE COUNTRIES ARE USEFUL CHECKS UPON THE ADMINISTRATION OF THE GOVERNMENT AND SERVE TO KEEP ALIVE THE SPIRIT OF LIBERTY. THIS WITHIN CERTAIN LIMITS IS PROBABLY TRUE—AND IN GOVERNMENTS OF A MONARCHICAL CAST PATRIOTISM MAY LOOK WITH ENDULGENCE, IF NOT WITH FAVOUR, UPON THE SPIRIT OF PARTY. BUT IN THOSE OF THE POPULAR CHARACTER, IN GOVERNMENTS PURELY ELECTIVE, IT IS A SPIRIT NOT TO BE ENCOURAGED.

The fight manifests in our broken congressional funding issues, which disrupt life in America too often. What if I said we could reduce our spending by up to 15 percent while simultaneously providing a better digital experience for Americans? I think that is a conservative figure; let me explain why.

We spend almost $2 trillion (or 30 percent of our budget) annually on technology projects.[48] I have been delivering technology for thirty years all over the world. In my private sector experience, more Agile approaches quickly result in half the cost and twice the value. That is just as true in the public sector.

I am not an economist, although while living in Norway, I developed much interest in macroeconomics, topics like purchasing power parity, tariffs, and the impacts of macroeconomic shifts and monetary policy. Unlike many Americans, I had the choice of which country to reside in, and I wanted to understand my options as a taxpayer; in my experience, that was challenging.

I once wrote an article for an expatriate magazine titled "Where Does the Money Go?" Many factors (i.e., currency strength and cost of otherwise public services on the private market) make comparisons difficult. However, I will offer a few observations, less from an economist's perspective than from a shopper of countries, admittedly my opinions. I think three significant factors reduce the return on the American taxpayer's investment compared with a lot of other countries, or at least Norway:

1. *We spend too much on defense and debt.*

U.S. defense spending increased by $71 billion from 2021 to 2022,[49] in part because of military aid sent to support Ukraine in its ongoing conflict, and the United States now spends more on defense than the combined ten countries listed by the Stockholm International Peace Research Institute.[50] Ironically, since we often overspend in this area, we end up financially overextended to many of the people we are supposed to be threatening (e.g., China).

2. *We spend money violently (in competition instead of community).*

In his Farewell Address, George Washington warned: "The alternate domination of one faction over another, sharpened by the spirit of revenge, natural to party dissension, which in different ages and countries has perpetrated the most horrid enormities, is a frightful despotism." Rank partisanship leads to transactional thinking, and more energy is spent staying in office or servicing political interests than assuring the general welfare of everyday Americans.

3. *We spend money inefficiently.*

Once laws are passed, and money starts to flow out into the bureaucracy, guided largely by the policy of violent legislators and fear, it is exhausted by broken systems and incentives. Besides cliché statements about thousand-dollar hammers, politicians do little to fix this. Here, instead, they often lay blame on the agencies or the staff of those agencies as cheap political tropes. Fear, helplessness, and self-interest flourish at the agency level because it comes with the funding. I will try to describe some of that below because this is where many great things can and are being done despite the politicians.

IS THE GOVERNMENT A BUSINESS?

It is easy for naysayers to blame government agencies and federal employees for the bloat and inefficiency resulting from dysfunction. Many people will then look to the private sector for answers. Why can businesspeople often run efficient and profitable companies with much higher customer satisfaction? Should we ask them to come and run our government?

On the surface, I understand this sentiment; perhaps that is what we need in Congress and running our agencies: someone who has gotten the job done in the private sector. According to the Brookings Institute, however, Congress is becoming increasingly occupied by former business leaders. In the 114th Congress, 231 members of the House and 42 senators identified as former business leaders (a nearly 150 percent increase since the 107th Congress).[51] It is my casual observation that neither the debt nor the institution's efficiency has improved over this period. So why are our business leaders also failing at running our country?

One crucial difference is that most companies exist to create value exclusively or predominantly for their shareholders, and they exist without the complex constitutional political structures that our framers introduced by design. The framers of our democracy, after all, did seek to limit the agency of our government. They had experienced oppressive governance, so perhaps they chose dysfunction as a design feature. I wonder if they meant it to be this bad or if it is wise of us to use this design flaw as an excuse to normalize bad-faith politics. However, it creates incentives that private business leaders have never faced.

In a typical shareholder model, customer satisfaction is important only as long as it serves the owners' bottom line. The U.S. government, on the other hand, is the property of the people it serves. Here, we, the people, are the shareholders and the customers, and the board of directors consists of partisan politicians with various conflicting interests besides the bottom line. A better comparison (although still deeply flawed) might be to a membership-serving enterprise like Costco. What could our government leaders learn from Costco?

As of May 2023, Costco had 124.7 million members.[52] Costco was the first company to grow from $0 in sales to $3 billion in sales in under six years.[53] My family spends almost one-third of our discretionary spending at this store or on their credit card. And we are not alone. Thirty-seven percent of Americans shop here, and, in my experience, most love it. As for me, I love it for four key reasons:

1. *I am getting a fair deal.*

They limit their profit and pass on the product of their purchasing power every time. They mark up their products at most 15 percent, producing a slight 2 percent profit.

2. *I value other humans.*

Using this meager profit, they take great care of their employees. They set a higher minimum wage, more full-time jobs, and better access to benefits.

3. *I am valued.*

They stand behind the quality of their products. My wife and I regularly return items, often clothing, because there are no dressing rooms. Still, they are friendly and ask few, if any, questions.

4. *I am supporting fair play.*

Executive compensation has always been comparably reasonable. While the current CEO makes more (still modest by industry standards), the founding CEO, Jim Senegal, kept his pay to a comparably moderate $350K and publicly stated that it was "wrong to have massive disparities between employee and executive pay."[54]

These ideas would be great for a government that is inclusive of all its citizens. We, too, should *all* feel seen, heard, and valued by *our* government. I want to benefit from economies of scale, for example, when purchasing necessary medications. I am happy if governments learn from Mr. Senegal but are cautious about other CEOs like Martin Shkreli, who was barred from his industry after marking up Daraprim from $13.50 to $750 per pill after obtaining exclusive rights to the decades-old drug.[55]

I welcome the wisdom of any business leader practicing an inclusive *stakeholder business model* that manages value in all forms, including but not limited to money, safety, esteem, equality, love, and belonging. This governance model argues the firm should serve the broader interests of stakeholders rather than those of shareholders only. These stakeholders include the enterprise's employees, clients, neighbors, environment, and community. This is a governance model designed to serve holistically and be sustainable. It's unfortunately rare in the United States, and where it does exist, like at Costco, it is often diluted after the founder leaves the business, as has been the case to some extent at Costco.

When any organization focuses too much on less relevant currencies (e.g., shareholder value), it is easy to lose track of the intrinsic ones (e.g., purpose, impact, or love). By design, my firm is stakeholder-driven. I remind my investors that they are stewards not only of the company but also of the values for which it stands, hoping this will delay the influence of extrinsic motivations when I leave.

I would love to see politicians come to Washington with truly intrinsic motivations, perhaps like the iconic James Stewart character in the movie *Mr. Smith goes to Washington* about a naïve, newly appointed U.S. senator who fights against government corruption. Many do come to change the world. We need those leaders, but they are rare, and I expect they will come from somewhere other than shareholder-driven companies.

Two types of problems are at play here: the ones I described earlier, which are primarily political and cultural. These problems (e.g., trust issues and fear) will never disappear entirely. Still, the antidotes (e.g., NVC, kindness, humanism, and willful interdependence) have already been discussed in this book. The other type of problem is structural. The good news is that many of the structural problems I am about to describe can be mitigated, and we are beginning to do so. I will explain that in the next chapter.

DON'T GO CHASING WATERFALLS

Perhaps the reader has heard the term "agile." Agile methodologies were developed in software engineering but have grown in prevalence since the 1990s to be used in all aspects of business. As the name suggests, the methodologies intend to be more agile about how we create products and services. It means that we reduce the amount of planning and predicting regarding what the user of our service or product needs and open better lines of real-time communication with our users. Once these lines of communication are open (we call them feedback loops), our next challenge is to be able to respond. In the past, long schedules have made this part challenging; what is the use in telling a user we will deliver upon their requirements but only when we can fit into the schedule behind the things they did not want? Agile exists in contrast to older models we in the industry have called the Waterfall.

THE WATERFALL METHOD

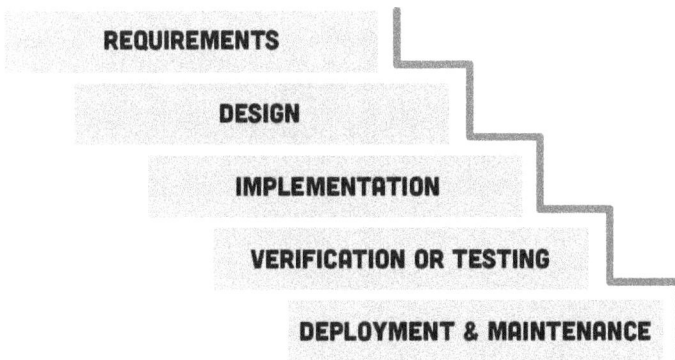

REQUIREMENTS

DESIGN

IMPLEMENTATION

VERIFICATION OR TESTING

DEPLOYMENT & MAINTENANCE

The Waterfall method is referred to as such because the activities are strictly organized in linear sequential phases, meaning they are irreversibly passed down onto each other, where each phase depends on the deliverables of the previous one and corresponds to a specialization of tasks. So, while the users are asked at some point what they want or need, those needs go into a planning process (perhaps for months), then into a design process (months more) and finally into a development process (yep, months more), then into testing (weeks perhaps), and finally out to the world where the user often has newer, more critical needs. Waterfall works fine for systems where needs rarely change, infrastructure is persistent (e.g., public water infrastructure or bridges), and technology is static (which are growingly rare). In such cases, we can predict what we will build and what technology will be available to make it. It still takes a long time to deliver.

But this is rarely a good solution for technology projects where new approaches emerge daily. Here, Agile approaches and tools often lower the cost of achieving and improving the outcome exponentially. Agile methodology is an alternative approach that breaks the project into continuous collaboration and improvement phases. Teams follow a constant cycle of planning, executing, and evaluating.

Waterfall is fine where algorithmic work is being done (e.g., in a manufacturing line), and workers are often production line or machine operators. But where creative, heuristic work is done, the static nature of the written and prescriptive requirements handcuffs the potential of the humans in the room to solve and design better outcomes as they work. Waterfall will reduce the cost of predictive algorithmic work; that is what Henry Ford did that sparked the industrial revolution. But for most technology projects, it will lead to exponentially higher costs even as it yields stale and dated outcomes. I could quote several studies concerning the failure rates of these projects.

However, Agile is, in my opinion, at least twice as efficient regarding costs and produces at least twice the value for the product or service user, simply because it leverages active feedback loops, follows the problems in the moment as they evolve, and applies available solutions as they evolve. The bottom line is that smaller, more agile, and iterative technology projects outperform Waterfall and deliver more value faster and for less money. And as technology is applied more widely, so are the efficiencies of this approach in other areas.

The good news is that our government is learning this lesson. Recent initiatives like those described in the next chapter have resulted in better outcomes. Our clients (e.g., the VA) are some of the most innovative and best stewards of technology I have worked with in the public or the private sector. As a result, they are seeing booming satisfaction rates.

However, they are still working with the constraints of the federal funding process. From a very high-level perspective, federal agencies deliver upon the direction of the executive and legislative branches of government in a very Waterfall-like method. First, the shareholders are courted in the political system as during the primary season, political platforms are presented by candidates for the executive and legislative branches, and then months later, these platforms are enacted after inauguration, but they must first be funded, and that itself takes months or years. So before we can get to our delivery problem described earlier, we are already keeping promises that are years old.

VIOLENT (COMPETITIVE) POLITICS

The priorities of the federal agencies are funded to implement the policies of the president and Congress. While the executive branch controls the nondiscretionary spending (about 73 percent), which is static and more predictable, Congress directly controls the remaining

27 percent.[56] It often uses that 27 percent as leverage to gain control of the 73 percent that the executive branch and its agencies need to stay in business.[57] In a mixed legislature, representatives from one party will usually use annual funding process to dismantle or disrupt the agenda of the other party.

This negotiation means that agency funding and priorities are handed down in a very Waterfall manner *when things work well.* These waterfalls, however, are often blocked by political maneuvering and intentional dysfunction. As George Washington predicted, the results are problems that would stump even Costco executives.

RISK AVERSION

The processes above are by design. Yes, the framers of our Constitution set much of this up this way. And sometimes, it feels that the inefficiencies are baked into their design. It takes a lot of work to describe the complexity of how ideas become laws, policies, and products or how long that takes to happen. It's like the product of Ibsen's sausage machine (quote at the beginning of this chapter). But the sausage machine is big and seems to run in a single direction. Most often, people who push back against the machine quickly learn that it is like sticking your finger into that sausage grinder; my first lesson as a federal contractor in DC was much like Mr. Smith's: if you don't respect that this machine has been running like this for almost 250 years, you are going to become another sausage. Good people told me this, and they were not wrong. I have learned to be skeptical of anyone who promises to dismantle the system that our framers built or to "drain the swamp." It is a naïve and ill-fated notion of populism, resulting only in more finger injuries.

So, the environment is one of extrinsic and unsafe spaces by design. Everyone feels helpless and threatened, and cortisol courses through the veins of leaders and followers alike. You can see this in the lit late-night office windows of public and private buildings alike in DC, as the work ethic is demanding. Something that shocked me upon exposure was the stereotype of lazy federal workers and politicians. They are by no means lazy, but they live in constant fear and helplessness. To question the often stale and outdated spending is to stick your finger into the machine.

This fear is reinforced daily as political appointees at all agencies inject the will of the elected president and of intolerant and violent politicians. If you recall, the requirements are set too far ahead because of the budget process and then interrupted repeatedly by congressional dysfunction (i.e., government funding battles, continuing resolutions, and failed budgets) that force frequent reprioritization. Add to this the regular election cycle, which can turn policies 180 degrees every two and four years, and it's genuinely unique that any project gets completed. Imagine yourself as a federal agency employee, working in this ecosystem, doing your best to apply the medical, legal, or technology degree you earned to help people and then being the victim of cheap stereotypes in the media. It's impressive that people stay in these jobs.

So, how does any work get done? Continuity is often reinforced through long-term contracts with the private sector. Once a project is awarded to a private party and funded via the government, it is usually in place for two to four years. It is almost impossible to stop it. To make things worse, it is also impossible to steer it. The project's product was often described in minutia via a "statement of work" or SOW. This document explains every project detail before the award ostensibly to hold the private partner accountable.

The problem with the SOW is twofold; first, it was written months or years in advance of the contract start, so the work to be done is probably based mainly on stale requirements and old technology stacks. The second problem is that it usually needs to be overly descriptive of how the work will be done. So, the buyer, who is often trained in acquisition, not technology, is charged to implement policy with technology is likely the least technically competent person and tells the technology company how to deliver their technology years before the project starts based on agency priorities that may be years old. How can this go right?

Thanks to our contracting professionals constantly spending what funds are available on approved projects, even if not relevant, our private sector will stay engaged with building things with little or no space or infrastructure for feedback loops. And thanks to better methodologies, they are making the wrong things faster.

I have taken liberties with that last remark to drive home my point. Fortunately, many innovative acquisition professionals and program managers work around the system's agency levels to mitigate this unacceptable situation. These heroes take personal risks to test the acquisition regulations, fire poor-performing vendors, and cancel or return funding streams (block the sausage). In my experience, they often work against the flow of their leadership, many of whom want to achieve the same outcomes but have been promoted by following orders. No one wins in this scenario, as great people came to the system to help people (Veterans get benefits, seniors get healthcare, a more robust economy is provided, safer aviation is enforced, etc.) and must take significant personal risks to mitigate the dysfunction of politicians who constantly use them as political fodder. In my work teaching Agile delivery, I have witnessed federal workers literally crying in my office. They came to their positions to serve value and want to do things right, but the machine is real.

CHAPTER TEN

BE THE CHANGE

I want us to ask ourselves every day, "How are we using technology to make a real difference in people's lives?"

—PRESIDENT BARACK OBAMA

DESIGNING WITH LOVE: A NEW APPROACH TO GOVERNMENT SERVICE DESIGN

Like many expats, I returned from Europe with a changed understanding of what government could and should be. As my story details, I fought these conclusions to the point of existential crisis. But in the end, I could not deny certain things. Among these conclusions was that wealthy and strong societies benefit when their citizens enjoy a certain amount of safety, compassion, and security. While I had left America as a staunch fiscal conservative, I was returning much less so.

I had lived and raised my children in a society where basic needs like healthcare and education were treated as necessities and rights. As a result, I was proud of what the Obama administration had achieved to introduce a fundamental step toward a similar future for Americans with the passage of the Affordable Care Act (Obamacare). With my new perspective, it gave me hope to see so much change, where a past version of myself would have perceived fear. I had come to believe in a more collective and compassionate government through experience, and I was now witnessing the emergence of that government through the sweat and love—yes, love—of many intelligent people.

In the last chapter, I spent a lot of time trying to dive into what is wrong with our government and to describe how futile it feels for those inside of it to make a difference. Now, I want to shed some hope and light on the story. Today, many wonderful people from other sectors have volunteered to scrub in, encouraging many from inside the system to take risks and make changes. There is much to be excited about, and these stories should be told more in the media. But it all started with a crisis.

THE LAUNCH AND COLLAPSE OF HEALTHCARE.GOV: A LESSON IN GOVERNMENT INNOVATION

Healthcare.gov was officially launched on October 1, 2013, to support the Obamacare legislation introduced in March 2010. This was to be the official website of the HHS to enroll millions of uncovered Americans in Obamacare. Problems with the website surfaced immediately as 250,000 people attempted to enroll in the first few hours. On the first day of service, only six Americans could register. An embarrassment for the Obama administration, the site's budget of $93.7M would eventually grow to $1.7B.[58]

> I'M GOING TO TRY AND DOWNLOAD EVERY MOVIE EVER MADE, AND YOU'RE GOING TO TRY TO SIGN UP FOR OBAMACARE. WE'LL SEE WHICH HAPPENS FIRST.
> —JON STEWART CHALLENGING KATHLEEN SEBELIUS (FORMER SECRETARY OF HHS) TO A RACE [59]

A movement that persists from the ashes of this disaster rose and is just getting off the ground eleven years later. Our largest federal agencies would learn to be lean to rescue this site and build upon those lessons. Start-ups within the government were formed and staffed by our nation's most innovative young designers and technologists. Entrepreneurs from Silicon Valley and all over the country rushed in to save the engine of Obamacare, perhaps the legislation itself, and then redefine how our government serves us.

In 2013, when the administration's key legislation was at risk and under extreme criticism for its ability to perform even a portion of its function, the White House chief technology officer (CTO), Todd Park, made several phone calls. Mickey Dickerson of Google answered the call and led the team that would work around the clock to restore the site and the confidence of the American people in a matter of weeks.

The following year, Dickerson would leave Google to take on the role of the first leader of a newly formed USDS. While Agile Six did not exist then, I have had the opportunity and honor to meet several people called in to serve their country, and we all should be eternally grateful. In their wake and at their example, today, thousands of technologists have answered the call to serve a time-limited *tour of duty* at USDS and/or as founders and employees of firms like mine at the federal, state, and local levels.

Without their fearless leadership and perhaps without the crisis of Healthcare.gov, many of us would not be doing this work today. In my opinion, one of the best things the Obama administration did was to create this federal component of the Civic Tech movement, the USDS, which is working to create opportunities for "tours of civic service." Their goals and focus are stated on their website: usds.gov.[60]

WE'RE SOLVING BIG PROBLEMS.

MILLIONS OF PEOPLE USE FEDERAL GOVERNMENT SERVICES EVERY DAY. VETERANS APPLY FOR HEALTHCARE, AND IMMIGRANTS APPLY FOR NATURALIZATION. TOO OFTEN, OUTDATED TOOLS AND COMPLEX SYSTEMS MAKE THESE INTERACTIONS CUMBERSOME AND FRUSTRATING.

TO IMPROVE THESE SERVICES, USDS HIRES MISSION-DRIVEN PROFESSIONALS FOR TERM-LIMITED "TOURS OF CIVIC SERVICE." WORKING ALONGSIDE CIVIL SERVANTS, THEY HELP ADDRESS SOME OF THE MOST CRITICAL NEEDS.

To institutionalize the lessons learned with Healthcare.gov, Dickerson and his team at USDS launched the *U.S. Digital Services Playbook*.[61] It is available today at playbook.cio.gov.[62]

This playbook, launched almost simultaneously to our business venture, would reaffirm and shape the company we would build. So much in this playbook resonated deeply with things I had learned from mistakes made in previous companies. Besides applying modern Agile methodologies, the addition of design thinking and data-driven decisions built upon much of what my customers needed. While I loved the federal clients I served, I became convinced they needed to find the budget and contractual structures to embrace these plays. And I so dearly wanted to do so!

DIGITAL SERVICE PLAYS

1. UNDERSTAND WHAT PEOPLE NEED.
2. ADDRESS THE WHOLE EXPERIENCE, FROM START TO FINISH.
3. MAKE IT SIMPLE AND INTUITIVE.
4. BUILD THE SERVICE USING AGILE AND ITERATIVE PRACTICES.
5. STRUCTURE BUDGETS AND CONTRACTS TO SUPPORT DELIVERY.
6. ASSIGN ONE LEADER AND HOLD THAT PERSON ACCOUNTABLE.
7. BRING IN EXPERIENCED TEAMS.
8. CHOOSE A MODERN TECHNOLOGY STACK.
9. DEPLOY IN A FLEXIBLE HOSTING ENVIRONMENT.
10. AUTOMATE TESTING AND DEPLOYMENTS.
11. MANAGE SECURITY AND PRIVACY THROUGH REUSABLE PROCESSES.
12. USE DATA TO DRIVE DECISIONS.
13. DEFAULT TO OPEN.

I wanted to use this playbook in the company I would create. I wanted to restore our government's relationship with its customers by designing federal service points with love. What do I mean by designing with love? If something is designed well, you can taste, feel, and believe in it. This goes for governments and how citizens experience them.

The fact that our political climate is so toxic and that opinion polls of our leaders are so low may mean we have a service design problem. It's time we look at these problems as consumers. When designing a consumer experience, it should be able to evoke a barista experience: "Here's a warm cup of coffee; now, what can I do for you?" It shouldn't just push you around.

For example, a few years ago, my wife was early to submit her ten-year renewal of her green card to USCIS (U.S. Citizenship and Immigration Services). For many valid reasons (i.e., the pandemic), USCIS was backlogged, and she was left in the dark, unable to get feedback or reassurance as it subsequently expired. Once her card officially expired the first time, she received an automatic extension for one year while the backlog was being managed. She could travel and reside in the United States for a year if she carried this letter with her expired green card. That worked until the letter also expired without a replacement; now, the renewal was one year late, and suddenly, she was in legal jeopardy to prove her residence was lawful. She could no longer travel, much less seek employment or a bank loan.

A second letter was not sent, and the USCIS refused to answer phone calls. The official policy on their website was to take calls only if clients were unusually late compared with everyone else, even if all applicants were already in legal jeopardy. She could only call or report the problem after about eighteen months expired. Again, recall that she submitted her renewal early. I don't know how seriously the agency leadership considered this inconvenience. But she and countless others could not obtain a job or loan because they could not prove legal residence; she could not travel home if a family member was sick. Some readers will appreciate, without an extended definition, that the Internal Revenue Service is currently in a very similar situation. If they owe you money, it will come when it comes; you cannot get an update or ETA.

We at Agile Six saw this as an opportunity to improve how government contractors could deliver these services by nurturing a sense of community rather than rivalry. But we knew we could not do this alone. There were only a few of us and a few hundred at USDS. So, we approached other like-minded companies to create the Digital Services Coalition (DSC) as a place for new start-ups to share knowledge, find teaming partners for government proposals, and mentor firms that want to get involved in rethinking how the government delivers digital services. By creating this community, we could all bring our best talents to the table and learn from one another's successes and failures. Together, we found ways to pierce the brick walls around the problems we wanted to fix, to make better sausage. If we don't have a budget, we ask for it. If we have too big a budget, we give it back. If we cannot make something better, we stay away. After all, it's our government; we believe in and love it.

People must love their work in this environment to do this kind of work. And they also must love their employer. Our mission as a coalition and community is to create a bubble of sorts. A self-sustaining anti-ecosystem within the toxic federal contracting ecosystem. Like an intrinsic ship sailing in extrinsic waters, we sought to face the sausage grinder together as a willfully interdependent community.

In the last chapter, we discussed the government's constitutional purpose: "to establish Justice, insure domestic Tranquility, provide for the common Defense, promote the general Welfare, and secure the Blessings of Liberty to ourselves and our Posterity."[63] The launches of USDS, DSC, and numerous state and local organizations, all with cultures supporting collaboration, NVC, and community activation for the public good, are restoring this constitutional role.

The Obama administration was the first to make this a critical part of their platform, introducing an Open Government Initiative based on transparency and civic engagement principles. The Memorandum on Transparency and Open Government (OGD)[64] highlighted three key areas that still animate our community:

1. *Transparent*

The government should be *transparent*. It must default to working in the open, showing its work and sharing its challenges. Today, the source code of many federal systems can be downloaded from repositories such as GitHub, and our teams work in the open, in front of the world.

2. *Participatory*

The government should be *participatory*. It is, of course, our government, as Abraham Lincoln stated at Gettysburg: "Government *of the people, by the people*, for the people."[65] Of course, this builds on the first principle of transparency: when people can see the work of their governments, they can more easily find a place to jump in.

3. *Collaborative*

The government should be *collaborative*. Agencies within local governments often solve the same problems, and building redundant systems is expensive and introduces expensive incompatibilities. Further, the private and public sectors should share lessons learned for their mutual benefit. Finally, vendors paid to solve government problems should collaborate (e.g., DSC) to solve joint problems for the citizens we serve.

TRANSPARENT GOVERNMENT

The directive starting this initiative (OGD) was issued on his first day in office on January 20, 2009. The bulk of the momentum that inspired us stems from this directive. It is a testament to how technological innovation can intersect with the democratic process to foster citizen empowerment. This period experienced a proliferation of open-source tools, digitally enhanced governance, and community participation in an unprecedented magnitude.

In a similar spirit, the OGD built upon the foundations of the Freedom of Information Act of 1966 (Johnson) and the Open Government Act of 2007 (Bush); taken in steps, these bipartisan initiatives formed the idea that information is the property of the society. Obama added that it should not simply be available because of complicated requests but, where possible, at the click of a button. It also served at local and international levels to solidify a new era of democratic governance based on the increased access that technology can provide.

Among the many international adaptations was the Open Government Partnership in 2011. This has undoubtedly led to more democratic governance globally as it now represents over two billion people, where governments have agreed to action plans that increase access to information through electronic means, resulting in greater accountability for political leaders and greater participation of the governed. Technology is improving governance, which is what we do at Agile Six and DSC. In the United States, our government's launch of the Data.gov platform in 2009 was a pioneering step in this direction, showcasing the government's commitment to transparency and engagement through open data.

PARTICIPATORY GOVERNMENT

The following decade saw an emergent Civic Tech, a field devoted to utilizing technology's power to promote civic engagement, improve government services, and create a bridge between citizens and their governments. Jennifer Pahlka launched the organization Code for America (CfA). This San Francisco–based nonprofit organization aims to make government for all people. In her 2012 TEDTalk,[66] Pahlka noted that we will not be able to reinvent government unless we also reinvent citizenship and asked, "Are we just going to be a crowd of voices, or are we going to be a crowd of hands?"

The motto of the CfA organization is:

We're people-centered problem solvers working to improve government in meaningful ways.

We're a passionate, mission-driven team that believes government at all levels can and should work well for everyone. Please get to know the people, showing that it's possible.

—Team CfA

Coding it Forward, launched in 2017, focused on integrating technology and government by providing fellowships to computer science students interested in public service. Initiatives like these increased talent supply in the civic tech sector.

COLLABORATIVE GOVERNMENT

For many people in many pursuits, the competition brings out their best. It is in besting someone else that some feel they can achieve their ultimate outcomes. Not us. I have heard many professional athletes and business leaders say that ultimately, the object of their competition is within themselves, that getting up every day to be the best version of themselves is the ultimate objective. While I understand this competitive spirit and have felt it, I have found more motivation in collaboration. I can compete against my rival, or I can compete against a problem (i.e., lousy government, healthcare delivery complexities, or contracting markets), and often my competitors become my allies.

Early in our journey, we started to question the need for rivals, for competition, and to put more energy into collaboration. I have seen the power of this kind of energy in generating more creative solutions and more authentic client trust. I have told many industry partners (most of whom could easily have been vicious rivals), "Let's get to know each other and what each other truly can offer; then you fly my flag, and I will fly yours; both will fly higher and brighter." We have several such stories, including our first prime contract and product inception, which was a client referred to us by one of our "rivals."

Our first partner would be someone with whom I developed an incredible admiration and mentorship. While she will never admit this, Dawn Halfaker is a true American hero in the sense that all of us can understand. She was wounded as a young Army officer in Iraq when her vehicle was struck by a rocket-propelled grenade. Dawn suffered the loss of her limb and many agonizing surgeries on the long road to recovery. When she reintegrated into civilian life, she founded her company, Halfaker & Associates, with the motto "Continuing to Serve."

Halfaker did serve and continues to do so, focusing much of its energy on strengthening the VA and supporting several other federal agencies in delivering healthcare integration. This was a very public side of Dawn's career that many saw. But more important to me was a side that fewer see: how she served other Veteran entrepreneurs.

I recall most keenly our first meeting between Ernie, myself, Dawn, and her senior team. We had just launched the business when she offered to sit with us. While there was nothing transactionally to be gained on her side, we flew across the country to honor this invitation. I recall a few critical things she said. First, as she walked into the room and started the conversation, she looked at me squarely in my eyes and said, "Robert, vet to vet (short for Veteran), I got your six; my success is your success." Dawn then gave me the best advice she had gained (at this point, I think she was already over 150 employees and expanding fast), including the advice to "never turn down a meeting," but most strikingly, I recall that she asked us for advice!

Key to our success was the spirit of "person to person" (an intentional expansion of Dawn's "vet to vet" approach); our success was always a joint success. We refused to form enemies or simple competitors but focused our energy on what partnerships we could build. When we lose to a "competitor," we endeavor (admittedly with frequent failure, especially in the beginning) to see loss as an opportunity to learn. We request debriefs from the clients who chose our competition, and we make friendly phone calls to the winners to congratulate them. This often led to future collaborations, but it always led to immediate lessons learned. It is not true that "to the victor go the spoils." It is infinitely more productive to own our failures and learn from them as the spoils of a "loss." It was in this spirit of collaboration above competition that the DSC was formed.

BUILD IT FAST OR BUILD IT RIGHT?

As I discuss the disruption of the federal IT space that our "movement" has led, I would like to lend a little perspective from my time before I entered this space. Some context is helpful for those unfamiliar with technology infrastructure or federal services, first on building fast versus building right (speed versus scalability). This is a classic trade-off few truly appreciate outside of the technology space, and many, even within the space, need more experience in both. Most start-up companies will focus on launching new services quickly to capture new markets. In contrast, more mature companies often acquire these start-ups and deal with long-term ownership and life-cycle management costs.

Before we judge our bureaucrats too harshly, it is essential to understand that the business of government is the ultimate challenge in ownership. Governments historically move slowly by design, and in the past, this has served us well.

Consider how many critical services we consume from the public sector in a single day. We awake to the lights of our homes, which consume electricity from a public grid; we check for news on the internet, which was developed by our government and is governed by public institutions; we consume safe food regulated by the Food and Drug Administration as aircraft pass overhead safely guided by Federal Aviation Administration regulated controllers and crew; we drink water and breath clean air (usually) safeguarded by the Environmental Protection Agency to drive on safe roads policed by public law enforcement and managed by our Department of Transportation to earn money in humane ways governed by the Department of Labor, which will be stored in Federal Deposit Insurance Corporation–supported banks.

The list goes on and on. The government is significant for a reason. We need these services to be more readily available and dependable than innovative. Innovation is fantastic, but for public services to be available and accessible, stability is critical. Therefore, it is often the role of our public employees and institutions to focus on ownership over innovation. They are not gamblers and are not necessarily focused on iterative experiments and celebrated failure. This has led to very stable but outdated systems.

As the pace of new technology accelerates, Silicon Valley and the technical start-ups that thrive there, on the contrary, are geared almost exclusively toward innovation. Often backed by extensive and speculative investments, they depend on getting their technology into the hands of early adaptors before the competition. They must service or even generate the appetites of technology consumers before their competitors. Long-term ownership issues can wait until someone else, a larger acquirer or a more mature division of the company, will sort those issues out later, often by rebuilding the entire code base more sustainably once a more mature user base is established. And if you are going to gamble on being first to market, you will lose often.

So, these teams limit the cost of development by creating what they call "minimum viable products." After all, there may be no appetite for the service, so we limit costs to test markets.

But these are yet to be critical services like air traffic control, clean water, or public healthcare infrastructure. Our government cannot experiment too loosely, or people die.

BUILD IT LOCALLY OR CENTRALLY?

In addition to the ownership versus innovation trade-offs, we often discuss centralization versus decentralization of resources. While there have been historical reasons to decentralize technology invest-ments (e.g., local knowledge and support of diverse work streams), the private sector has been moving toward centralizing IT resources throughout my career (thirty years at least). For many reasons (both political and technical), this trend has not kept up in the public sector.

I have mentioned previously that my digital experience with my government while living in Norway was far superior. This was primarily due to centralizing information systems and technology investments into fewer public sector entities. This is a complex political and technical issue considering many factors, including embedded hierarchies of systems and people. But it is growingly expensive and inefficient for every federal, state, and local agency to host their systems. Technology resources are more centralized in Norway and many other countries (perhaps more so in smaller countries).

Since 2008, Norway has developed and evolved its ALTINN solution, a public sector–wide platform for collecting and storing sensitive information and forms. This enables, among other things, a single point of authentication and data storage and security across all public sector services and a single standard of usability. While in the United States, most agencies manage disparate technology teams, Norway has long focused on centralizing IT resources and experi-ences. Since 2018, they have had a dedicated minister of digitalization concentrating on critical metrics tracking Usability, Transparency, and Mobility.[67] This is close to the priorities in the Open Government Directive (Transparency, Participation, and Collaboration).[68]

The Presidential Innovation Fellowship (PIF) program solved much of the above by creating two agencies. In 2012, the PIF was implemented, modeled after CfA, and brought eighteen top innova-tors from the public sector to team with federal innovators to introduce a private sector mentality, more innovation, more experimentation, more centralization, and so on. As it matured (made permanent in 2017), this group of innovators launched the two new "start-ups" we have discussed within the government in 2014 to institutionalize what it was learning, the USDS would champion innovation, and the 18F would handle ownership and centralization.

Housed within the president's executive office, the USDS provides consultation service to federal agencies. Former president Obama has described it as a technology SWAT team.[69] Attributed to the idea of Jennifer Phalka (founder of CfA) and, at the time, CTO of the United States, Mikey Dickerson, the former Google engineer who had been instrumental in rescuing Healthcare.gov, would serve as its first head. As we have worked with this team and as I have experienced it, their role is to deploy into the federal agencies and help inject new thinking focusing on the administration's priorities but making it safer to experiment with innovation.

Alternatively, and by design, 18F enjoys more political separation from the administration's priorities. Thinking more long-term about innovation issues, they reside within the General Services Administration, an independent agency charged with supporting the general needs of all federal agencies. This makes sense since their role is more about tackling the long-term inconsistencies among all federal agencies (versus only those with current political pressure).

They do this mainly by implementing products developed by USDS, including the *Digital Services Playbook* (playbook.cio.gov), a brief description of thirteen "plays" critical to how technology is built and delivered, the U.S. Web Design Standards, a description of designs and standards to improve the accessibility and design congruency of digital experiences and the common learnings about how to acquire these services from the private sector as presented in the "TechFAR," a guide to how to work within the federal acquisition regulations and a training program for contracting officers. With these tools, 18F enables willing agencies to procure, build, and support better performance, usability, scalability, and cost solutions.

BUILD IT FOR PROFIT OR PURPOSE?

So far, I have discussed the practical trade-offs of public technology development (fast versus right, innovation versus ownership, and centralization versus decentralization). However, here, I can speak more freely as a private citizen, and the DSC has spoken more openly as a community about the private sector's motivations in this community.

To spend the public's money is a sacred service. We must always remember that public trust is not easily earned and is quickly lost. And so it is that I have taken a lesson from my mentor, Dawn Halfaker, in saying human to human, "I got your six; my success is your success." We have chosen, therefore, as a community, both in Agile Six and at the DSC (and I believe this is widely true in the Civic Tech space at large), that we "are stronger together," and this, in my opinion, is the manifestation of nonviolent collaboration (the DSC Manifesto):[70]

COMMUNITY OVER CREDIT

EACH WIN MOVES US ALL CLOSER TO DIGITAL
TRANSFORMATION.

PURPOSE OVER PROFIT

WE'RE MISSION-DRIVEN, NOT MONEY-DRIVEN.

USERS OVER STAKEHOLDERS

IF WE DON'T MEET USER NEEDS, BUSINESS GOALS
WILL NEVER BE MET.

INNOVATION OVER RISK MANAGEMENT

CHANGE COMES FROM TAKING CHANCES.

OUTCOMES OVER ACTIVITIES

SUCCESS IS WHAT YOU ACCOMPLISH, NOT HOW MUCH
YOU DID TO GET THERE.

DELIVERY OVER DELIBERATION

PERFECTION ONLY EXISTS ONCE USERS TELL YOU
IT'S PERFECT.

I hope that this chapter has given you some hope. If you are a technology builder, please visit our community and check out the coalition (DSC) website (digitalservicescoalition.org), the USDS.org website, or any of our coalition partners (listed on the site above). We are constantly hiring nonviolent people who wish to do more than build careers; they want to feed people, be a part of inclusive communities, restore the agency of our public sector, and make a difference.

If this is not you, please at least see the change for what it is: an attempt to stop pulling at the same old fishing line knots, an honest effort to untangle the digital parts of our democracy.

CHAPTER ELEVEN

INCLUSION IS OUR PRODUCT

Inclusion is not a matter of political correctness. It is the key to growth.

—JESSE JACKSON

Dan Levenson was a turning point in many ways. He was our first customer, and he became our first champion. So, it was natural at some point when he grew increasingly frustrated with federal employment that we joined forces. He would become like the fifth founder, joining our company first as a strategist and eventually assuming the role of president and my trusted sparring partner. The timing of his arrival was also the genesis of an identity shift. Like the individual in Maslow's hierarchy, our basic collective needs were being met, as were many of our higher needs. We had steady revenue, and we were now about twelve employees. It was time to transcend as a collective, become more of us, and commit more deeply to what was alive in us.

This meant shifting our focus from the larger community of federal "GovCon" contractors to our heart's most authentic desires, the burgeoning Civic Tech space. We stopped taking phone calls from the more prominent traditional players. With integrity, we backed out of work that did not align and started seeking leadership opportunities in places where it did. As the reader will understand, I would very much like to say that we made no compromises getting to this place; after all, I have harped on and on about the need for authenticity. But here is where existential flexibility comes in. It is unfair to say we jumped straight into the Civic Tech space without trying to play in both worlds. I hope you understand that we had to meet our deficiency needs first (cash flow), and I lost a lot of sleep along the path.

But Dan never experienced that season. As soon as he came on board, these kinds of compromises stopped. We walked away from millions of dollars of pending work (a few stories I could tell in another book) and refocused on being us. Dan and I also focused on fixing the system around us so that others who came behind us could skip the low road altogether. Together with fifteen other firms, we launched the DSC to remove the barriers we encountered and attract better and more collaborative competitors. We wanted to pave the road for others so that they did not have to experience this season of compromise in the same way we did.

Initially, the DSC better reflected our vision than our own website. The energy it brought into the space was (and still is) genuinely game-changing. As we sat with other founders and employees in our space, we learned that we could reset the table together. We found partners and competitors who, like us, built things around Americans and, with few exceptions, openly shared information, tools, and even source codes. My vision was of engineers on separate projects and from different companies openly sharing their time and talents for the common good. And this still is more often the case than not. I am genuinely warmed when it goes to one of our coalition partners if we lose a bid. In this scenario, we congratulate them and then try to learn from what they accomplished for the next round of competition. I count these "competitors" among my closest friends. Business is personal—at least, it should be.

Free of the constraints of government, Dan continued to unfold new relationships, methods, and people. His passion is for this movement and reforming the landscape of federal acquisition. He served as the first president of the DSC. For much of his first few years at Agile Six, he spent more time supporting the coalition and offered free advice to buyers and competitors alike. He has also mentored many new entrepreneurs and transitioning federal employees. He gives freely of his time and energy wherever he sees the opportunity for change. For me, he became a more intelligent and younger protégé; to others, a giving mentor. Eventually, both his siblings joined our collective, and his sister Emily would be at least as transformational in a completely different way.

The tagline to our logo is "Better place to work. Better work to do." If Dan is the champion of "better work" (innovative federal clients), Emily Levenson became the architect of "better place to work." Her background as an attorney brought an immediate sense of security when she came on as our general counsel. Still, her disposition (passion for people and wise temperament) rapidly shifted her focus to building our new culture.

We decided very early that we would never have managers or sales goals. We would grow only so fast as people arrived and self-actualized in our collective (unfolded as autonomous and authentic self-managed professionals). We soon had plenty of customers lined up to whom we made commitments, never outgrowing or outpacing our ability to deliver. We see both our work and our people as sacred obligations; the alignment of the people and the work is the only driver of growth.

Neither are places to compromise for the sake of profit. I truly believe they both know this. So, with Emily's help, we focused on building a scalable system, with our growth never outpacing the development of our culture.

Four men founded a company together and added a fifth. What could go wrong? Entrepreneurs often jump into business like I did by calling the most intelligent people they know. This was by necessity, but I cannot overstate the blind spots we had and still have. From her first day, Emily got to work on those. We brought in external experts to conduct surveys and provide input on recruiting techniques and human policies. We set up a diversity, equity, and inclusion (DEI) lab where gracious volunteers spawned the work of inclusion, eventually influencing the books we read and how we spoke to one another. Amazingly, we have attracted some diversity despite our ignorance, and I must applaud the leadership of all these people. They came in attracted by our mission despite our lack of diversity and made it a safer place for others.

I wish I was the one who had championed inclusion or even understood what it meant. In fact, for a long season in this story, words like "diversity," "equity," and "inclusion" scared me. I can recall experiencing existential fear and even thoughts of selling the company during times when fear would rise within me. You see, it's tough for us to see our privilege, and when others start to point it out, it's not easy to ingest for our egos. The Jackal gets really loud. How could someone call me privileged? I just told you all my story!

So, I must admit that inclusion work was incepted at first as a gesture of compliance. What felt like a liability would become our greatest asset! I understood intellectually that bias existed and that diversity was essential to our clients and staff. However, I needed to understand that diversity absent inclusion is cruel and that inclusion takes work from those with power and privilege. An analogy I came across is that it is unkind to ask someone to a party but not ask them to dance. We must build a diverse workforce and an inclusive culture so that everyone feels seen, heard and valued. No wallflowers.

So, we started the inclusion work with half of my heart involved. Our consultants performed a survey that would break that half. I heard in no uncertain terms from this survey that I needed to do the work of inclusion better. While our collective had attracted some women, those women told me through this survey that they did not feel heard. They attributed this to good intentions but a lack of invest-ment on my part to understand. I was reading the wrong books and quoting the wrong people in my leadership talks. Who were they to tell me that Maslow was a white dude? They were entirely correct.

For a brief season, my Jackal raged, and I let violent language into my heart, I alternated between self-judgment and ego, and I felt I was being told I did not belong in my own company. After all, who would tell me what to read or think? I was the founder. I had a blind spot the size of the Grand Canyon. I wrestled for weeks with my ailing Jackal voice. I now know without doubt that the women in our company were sharing their experiences with me out of trust and love.

They served me the greatest compliment I have ever received by trusting me with the truth. After all, it was my company; I was safe, and they took all the risk. And further, they were speaking and taking risks for identities even more underrepresented. As these women pushed for change and worked to feel safe, they also made space for others. I will admit that I sat for hours in tears with a report over one hundred pages long. It had many beautiful things to say, but I did not hear much. What broke my heart was that I was being called human, and I assumed I was being labeled as biased and uninformed. No one called me mean, questioned my intentions, or even pointed out that my work thus far was primarily motivated to check a box. They had just pointed out that I was human and needed help.

Thankfully, my dear friend Emily was gracious enough to walk me through this season without bullshit. She showed empathy and spoke to my needs, but she did not sugarcoat or hide the truth. Neither did she back down from it. Together with many other champions of change, we started the unending work of doing better. Today, we work to do better, and when we succeed, we blossom in unimaginable ways. But no box has been checked, and no compliance has been met because the work of being human and seeing others as human is never complete. Bias and the Jackal will always be in the back room, waiting to jump out and sabotage love.

I will make a few points to give credit where it is due. NVC was introduced into our culture by a Sixer—a woman with a passion for creating positive change. Another Sixer, also a woman, who is one of the most talented Agile coaches I know, turned me on to Teal and Frederic Laloux. Our DEI labs, book clubs, and people operations team are increasingly diverse and representative of those we serve. These humans have opened new doors for increasing our voice, making it safe for me to admit my mistakes and for others from historically disadvantaged groups to join our collective. With their help, I have realized that nonviolent communication is the language of inclusion and that diversity should only be built upon a foundation of equity and inclusion.

I mentioned earlier that love impacts our product. As we embraced inclusion, we were able to support more diversity and put a lot of effort into equal pay (covered in the next chapter). The net result is that everyone felt safer, free to be authentic, and more gratified. At the individual and collective levels, needs were satisfied, including safety, esteem, and belonging. While this is an ongoing effort, the product has already benefited; we have heard from our clients that our teams are more transparent, that they have an unheard-of resilience, and that their users can feel the outcomes of our inclusion. We have attracted employees from inside and outside our space who have come to us intentionally to be a part of our collective and to have authentic expression.

To the extent that we have genuinely embraced DEI, Teal, and NVC, we are becoming the baristas of great things. Our business grows in total revenue, talent density, and the quality of our clients as measured by the trust and autonomy they return to us. I want to be very clear that inclusion is our product. We build better by putting people first, and the diversity of those people is directly responsible for the inclusion of the users of our products.

I meet every new Sixer when they arrive; I do this in small groups with a few critical messages. I emphasize the story in this book; I give them my commitment to their wholeness and challenge them to do the same with kindness. I protect what we have built and warn them against injury to the collective. I let them know with certainty that we will have their six through many challenges, but our values are non-negotiable—disrespect them and lose your position in our company.

CHAPTER TWELVE

HOLDING THE SPACE

It's not the notes you play; it's the notes you don't play.

—MILES DAVIS

Our culture manifests as we implement our values. In our case, these values are currently (and we keep these open to evolution) trust, wholeness, self-management, purpose, and inclusion. However, are these always the authentic highest values of all our people? Are they even my current highest values? We all encounter life in seasons, and if we are honest with ourselves, our values shift slightly at the individual and collective levels. I have worked in organizations where people are measured annually for how well they reflect the companies' values (often set in stone at founding) and how well they "perform" based on those values. This is in my opinion inorganic and inauthentic and, while good-intentioned, can detract from potential growth and wholeness.

As an ideal, we agree to our values when we are hired and pursue them every day. We also agree that they are evolutionary, and if they fail to reflect the collective, they can evolve. There is a paradox here, though, as we must balance this evolution with some level of stability. We could spend endless hours otherwise in discussions and debates trying to resolve daily the will of the collective at every minute level, including both the employees and the owners of the firm. This can lead to paralysis. So, as much as we strive to create as flat of an organization as is practical, we do sustain a minimum hierarchy. As the founder and majority shareholder, I am the ultimate arbitrator of our values. These values are deeply informed by our employees and implemented by our executive core (four people currently). Other than them, no one in the company is charged to manage others.

I prescribe to the advice Fredric Laloux gave in his book *Reinventing Organizations* that the key role of a CEO is in holding the space so that teams can self-manage.[71] It means keeping others, like investors and executives, from screwing things up. I have invited other investors along the way after careful screening and with the clear understanding that they are stewards of the company until our employees ultimately own it. To this end, we have established an employee stock ownership plan (or ESOP). Annually, the investors set goals by which excess profit (profit driven by exceptional collective performance and savings of self-management) is returned to the cooperative (in equal portions) in the form of equity in the ESOP trust. I dream that one day, the company will be 100 percent employee owned.

> **EFFECTIVE ORGANIZATIONS COMPENSATE PEOPLE IN AMOUNTS AND IN WAYS THAT ALLOW INDIVIDUALS TO MOSTLY FORGET ABOUT COMPENSATION AND INSTEAD FOCUS ON THE WORK ITSELF.**
> **—DANIEL PINK**

Meanwhile, my role as the CEO is to "hold the space,"[72] as Laloux describes it. To me, this has two essential functions. First, I must continue to unfold my founding vision for the company, which includes room for neurodiversity, evolution, and open discussion. Second and in support of this, I must be the ultimate arbitrator of our values via our policy. For a long season, I found this challenging.

The egalitarian values of Jante have grown in me, and my humility has sometimes prevented me from pressing my values upon the collective. But at some point, I realized that the collective needs an ultimate arbitrator, hopefully, one that will genuinely listen with an open heart, check ego, and maximize their voice. After all, people in different seasons and different backgrounds will still disagree. As an enterprise with a job to do, people need clarity. The following are some points of "clarity" where we are pretty different from other firms.

Several of our employees have sometimes expressed admiration and frustration with these policies, which is understandable. To me, these are often about sustaining a nonpaternal, nondominating culture. It requires all of us to discard much of what we have learned including engrained thought patterns. Most of my energy has been in pushing back as traditional ideas like individual performance-based compensation, quarterly goals, sales targets, or strategic planning seem to seep in at every corner. It's only natural that as we grow, new people with great intentions bring their experience to the problems we face. So, in a way, "holding the space" becomes about keeping us weird and reminding people why we are weird.

EMERGENT STRATEGY AND SENSE AND RESPOND

For most of my career, I could be labeled as a project manager. I was taught to plan and stick to that plan. Indeed, I have experienced some success with this thinking. As certified project management professionals, we were taught to create extended, detailed plans, and we were tested in the ability to "monitor and control" people and resources to achieve these plans. I recall war rooms with walls covered in extended detailed plans. We had tools that color-coded the phases, dependencies, and critical paths to success. I hope I am not the first to confess that these plans *never* came to fruition the way I thought they would. In fact, much of my energy was spent replanning (or "re-baselining") and adjusting. If I am honest, the artifacts were mainly produced to solicit funding from project sponsors and trust from senior managers.

I cannot count the number of times good ideas were tossed out or delayed simply because they would cause too much disruption to this false security system. Like this approach, we encounter many similar well-intentioned tools, such as objectives and key results. At Agile Six, we have tried a few of these tools. While I do not mean to discount their value for many organizations, we have found them expensive, inorganic, and potentially obfuscatory.

For me, business execution comes in the form of emergent and deliberate strategy. Many organizations will lean more on the deliberate approach I have discussed earlier, and we do plan for some things.

But we have seen a lot more opportunities to embrace what emerges in our environment than what we expected to emerge. This is a dynamic Laloux describes as "sense and respond."[73]

"Sense and respond" is an approach that requires a great deal of trust and wholeness in the collective organization. It seeks as a goal to listen more than we talk. A sensory organization is one in which all voices are sources of new ideas and improvements, requiring, by nature, an inclusive community and, instead of leaders, setting directions far in advance for the quarter, year, or longer, everyone in our organization is a leader.

Leaders listen to clients, to colleagues, to their own inspiration daily and maximize the organization's ability to respond to what they hear. Much like the Agile Manifesto that prioritizes people over process or response over planning, we lend more credence to what arises within us than what we expected. We still have delivery coaches and business strategists who maintain a minimum level of planning. But as CEO, I have no interest or role in reviewing or approving these plans. My job is to listen to the collective, to the market, and to my own inner voice to inform these people in what they do, not direct them.

I never tell them what to do, and we do not set growth or sales targets. As stated earlier, we focus instead on growth impediments, mostly on how fast we can recruit and properly support great people and clients. Our organic outcomes are considered more than enough; our investors must always accept that.

WELL-INTENTIONED PATERNALISM

I mentioned in the previous paragraphs that some people feel frustrated operating in our environment and that old thought patterns need to be abandoned. Foremost among those patterns is the deeply seated instinct of paternalism. I am not saying that we should not practice this instinct at home; it certainly is the foundation of great parenting. But I have come to believe we need to leave it at home.

Earlier in this book, we discussed the need for gratification and how, as children, we attached to our parents as our first source of needs. Culture may then influence the conditions to which our early attachments are governed. In many cultures, children are taught varying levels of deference to parents. Sometimes subsequent attachments can be likewise transactional and governed by rules such as "respect your elders"; we learn to formally address our teachers and even senior colleagues. "Superiors" in these relationships have historically been charged also with the application of extrinsic motivation (punishment, rewards, assessment, and praise) in order to advance the development of the "inferior" identity.

I believe these forms of transactional and conditional service of needs only stunt emotional growth and transcendence for both parties. They lend themselves to egoic reinforcement and unhealthy dependencies. I am not here to question anyone's parental techniques, although I regret some of what I did with my children. However, I wish to examine if that attachment should persist past adolescence and especially into the workplace.

In my experience, paternal instincts have been our most challenging forces in building a less hierarchical company. As members of our culture and experienced managers, parents, or even siblings, it's tough to refuse the paternal role. Most often, as employees, we have become accustomed to it, so we request or demand it. My project manager or people manager career has served me well in organizations to create followers instead of leaders. And I have been guilty of looking to mentors as father or mother figures and developing an appetite to serve in such roles.

So, I understand when this continues to creep up in our organization. The typical model is that compensation is set by managers who assess the performance of *their* people. However, I firmly believe that self-actualization and individual ego transcendence start where paternalism ends. One could write—and some have written—an entire book on the negative impact of paternalism (and the patriarchy that sustains it in culture), but I will give a few examples of how we have endeavored to hold these appetites at bay.

PASS/FAIL EMPLOYMENT

We hire great people, pay them well, and get out of their way. This means we reject performance appraisals, especially in the traditional sense. We know this is a trade-off as we often hear that people would like feedback. And feedback is essential, so we direct people instead to get it from their peers. We do not wish nor feel qualified to give this feedback when we are distant from their work, simply based on our seniority. The next question is usually, "How would you like me to do that?" Without managers, long-term goals, or detailed and static values, there is little to no infrastructure to "measure" someone's performance objectively.

And I would posit that most such measures are ultimately subjective to a manager's personality, proximity, appetites, and other factors. For our part, we consider people successful so long as we don't hear anything else. We consider them equal as well, and we compensate them as equally as we can. Of course, we have challenges and infrastructure for repair of ruptures, remediation of issues, and even termination.

> THE FUNDAMENTAL INSIGHT IS THAT WITH US,
> TRUST IS GIVEN BY DEFAULT AND LOST BY
> INDIVIDUAL ACTION.

EQUAL PAY FOR EQUAL WORK

We have mostly systemized our pay system. We openly advertise our pay rates in hiring PDs based on how a project was sold (i.e., what the customer paid for). All people doing the same role can be assured that they earn within 2.5 percent of their peers. This is reinforced with both an algorithmic system and an annual review/audit by a dedicated equity review team. This is not based on years of service, past performance, or education, all potentially subjective factors. And suppose we cannot hire someone from the market in the pay range that others get. In that case, we increase the range and move every existing employee in the same role to the new negotiated rates. Further, we have regular equity reviews of this system and sustain a rupture reporting system for individuals to appeal the outcomes (as even the most impartial systems can fail). Promotion in our pay system is only possible (after hire) by applying for and receiving a new and more demanding position in subsequent projects. No managers, no politics.

AUTOMATIC PAY RAISES

We decided long ago to try to keep money out of our daily discussions. The only way to do that fairly is to pay people well and keep it so. Recall that we have no metrics to decide who gets more than whom, so we do the best we can for everyone. I have participated in traditional annual processes that use countless hours and political maneuvering to assess everyone in a firm to support debates between ill-informed managers about who "deserves" larger or smaller portions of the budget. It is my growing sense that these are managed inequities.

Since we have neither infrastructure nor desire to rank our colleagues, we give everyone the same. If results support us, this has worked out to 5 percent per year—half automatically in the summer and half at the end of the year as long as we are profitable, and it won't injure anyone (e.g., cost someone a job or reduce ESOP payouts). This took some faith as we can only escalate our prices to our clients by 2–3 percent per year. But our employees have always found ways to increase our margins or control costs in such a way that we achieve these raises without friction and are still able to add generously to our employees in the form of profit sharing, 401(k), and ESOP contributions, all of which are primarily funded by the savings involved in *not* sustaining the infrastructure to manage inequities.

SELF-MANAGEMENT FOR REAL

In support of employee autonomy, we are increasingly looking for new ways to move decisions to them (where the information is). Upon hire, all employees are given a credit card and encouraged to be fiscally responsible and buy what they need. Advice on purchases is provided by peers via an advice channel (via Slack).

Still, no approval is required for office equipment, travel, or social expenses with colleagues. For professional development, we provide guidance based on historical spending and advise them on the tax implications of certain decisions. Further, where projects allow and collaborate with their teammates, we do not set office hours or require any specific place or time of work. Suppose an employee needs help with these responsibilities. In that case, we provide one-on-one support through a self-management coach but never permission or direction.

WELLNESS DAYS

Again, where projects allow and in collaboration with their teammates, we provide employees an unlimited budget of wellness time. This is intended to help employees show up whole. It is to protect PTO (paid time off) for vacation and sustain a balanced life. Employees are the best judge of their wellness, and we want them to show up whole and inspired. So, it's OK to "call in sad." As with all our policies, abuse will often manifest in the teams, and we support teams to hold one another accountable to excellent outcomes.

Teams usually surface issues after they have tried to resolve them, and if someone is not pulling their weight, it will result in a "fail" in our system and rather quickly a termination. It is up to the Sixers themselves to navigate and negotiate the conditions of success in their teams. We trust they will follow our values and most often succeed. Our values also guide the teams to be compassionate and allow for seasons of hardship without injuring the client or the collective. Here, we keep training such as NVC, Agile, and Inclusion and coaches to facilitate dialogues.

COLLECTIVE ACCOUNTABILITY AND STEWARDSHIP

I am often asked, "But who is accountable for *X*?" I understand this in the traditional sense that someone must be held accountable. However, we firmly believe individual accountability is not as strong as collective accountability. So, we lean on that. All our employees know that their decisions impact one another. Unnecessary expenses reduce ESOP contributions (dollar for dollar), poor customer service or delivery limits our growth and thus opportunities for advancement, violent communications reduce all our experience at work, and so on.

Upon employment, I tell people, "Don't fall down in a crowded room. Ask for advice, but then do what you think is right. We will all have your back, even if it turns out wrong." I find that much like a buffet on a cruise ship, we learn to moderate our appetites if we believe that resources are abundant. And I have seen people act exponentially more accountable to peers than they would to managers.

COMPASSIONATE GIVING

We offer and require all employees to attend training to make them better teammates. NVC, Agile, and Inclusion (e.g., rupture and repair) courses empower us to share the abundant resources in "the buffet" with one another in self-organized teams. We learn to recognize and feed what lives in one another and empower colleagues to transcend. This is not simply conflict resolution (although it helps) but the tools required to see, hear, and value one another. To ensure that this is happening, we regularly conduct surveys and elicit open feedback. But, most importantly, we make ourselves available to listen and provide advice (never permission or direction).

TRANSPARENT AND STRAIGHTFORWARD BUSINESS INFORMATION

We have worked hard to simplify our business. While some of our colleagues in finance may look deeper on occasion, for the most part, we manage our business with three numbers. The scorecard is shared throughout the company every month. It includes net profit (month and year) influencing our ESOP payments, employee balance (monthly), and customer satisfaction (sporadically as available). Aside from these simple gauges, you won't find any corporate performance data circulating in our ranks (outside of finance, who keep our cash flow positive).

Everyone knows the score, and we work as a team to improve all three factors, measured only against the previous month and year. We must realize as a team that these factors influence each other. If net income is too high, employee or client satisfaction suffers and vice versa. Every employee senses and responds in their own way to these figures, not to any arbitrary goal set from an ivory tower. Of course, we all feel the impact of all of them. If we are unhappy, we feel it; if we are unprofitable, we feel it (all of us, thanks to ESOP); if our customers are unhappy, we feel it. So, as a collective, we move to maximize our values, not to produce a particular outcome at the expense of others.

RESPECTING THE SEASONS (EBB AND FLOW)

I would love to promise all our employees that the pace of work will be stable and there will be no long days. The facts of our business (and most) do not support this. In reality, we often have long days and demanding seasons. But we find that some relief can and must be found in the ebbs and flows of life. So, I tend to reject calendars, goals based on them, or maturity standards imposed externally. Such artificial constructs impede periods of rest.

With no managers running around trying to remove inefficiencies (e.g., idle employees) or mature infrastructure (e.g., maturity models), people can feel safe to relax or go home early when things are not busy. It feels like a sacred contract with salaried employees who do not receive overtime that we make reasonable faith efforts to smooth out the workload and then respect the ebb and flow of seasons.

It is the least we can do not to make them feel unsafe when things slow down. Of course, long-term business contraction is a more challenging issue. We face the occasional redundancy, but I think it's much less often. We endeavor to avoid it because our staff are safe and inspired to create new opportunities, especially when they are balanced and happy. When we expect and assume new work will replace or expand old work, it tends to happen. When we fear and prepare for contraction, it tends to happen.

In summary, my job is to create and hold the space for trust. We have had hundreds of people apply for each of our roles, and we meticulously vet them for capability and disposition. But once they are hired, they are trusted by default. Trust is not something they need to earn nor sustain via politics, proximity, or overperformance. We do not compare them or measure them against one another. Instead, they will unfold authentically and yield the best possible product for our teams and our government. They are held accountable to their teams, and we are held responsible collectively.

But working for us is not a fairy tale. People do leave us, both by choice and termination. But not for failure of paternalism or politics. Most often, they see new agencies in other places, and their seasons shift, and we celebrate that. We are not trying to be on the top of anyone's "Best Places to Work." Not everyone thrives in this environment. We want to be the most authentic fit for people who do (like me).

Trade-offs are admittedly many; we often lack the maturity of structure, and advancement can be stunted, especially if management is your passion. There is always some sawdust on the shop floor when we work out loud and in the open. Some come for a season (perhaps of rest) and then retreat to more traditional companies with more conventional career ladders. Long-term people tend to be more post-egoic, post-economic, and ready to work to live (with purpose and quality) versus live to work.

CONCLUSION

Animals live that impersonal and universal life without knowing its nature. Ordinary people know its nature and don't live it and, if they think seriously about it, refuse to accept it.

An enlightened person knows it, lives it, and accepts it completely. He eats, drinks, and in due course he dies—but he eats with a difference, dies with a difference.

—ALDOUS HUXLEY, *ISLAND*

As I write the conclusion of this book, I am in my wife's hometown of Vennesla, Norway. It has been our custom since moving back to the United States to spend most of our vacations here. Most recently, I have had the opportunity to work from here for weeks and enjoy the mild Norwegian summers. I have had a hard time explaining why this is increasingly important to me.

It has become a pilgrimage to a place where language is less violent, people are less competitive, and communities are more collective. It's a respite from the uber-competitive and increasingly resource-scarce

America. It would have been irresponsible of me not to try to share what I have found. And even if I wanted to hide here in Norway, the forces of violent, individualist, competitive, and inhumane language also exist here and grow louder as time passes, partially at least as foreign influences arrive.

As we arrive at the end of this book, I thank you, the reader, for reading my story. I never thought I would be the kind of person to write a book. Why was I so open to rethinking everything I had known? I once was told that identities are like tethered buoys in the ocean. The buoys are set during our upbringing and early childhood and then reinforced by our communities. Our ideological upbringing is like cement anchors deep under the water and, to keep the buoy functional, are designed not to move. Like buoys, our visible ideology may shift left and right, but our upbringing anchor is always tethered to keep them from moving too far.

Indeed, our worldviews often will vary within a tolerable distance of where our parents and caregivers planted them unless drastic events shift the very sand beneath them. When the anchor is moved, perhaps because of trauma or significant change in communities, we can see drastic changes. Most people only shift anchors a few times in life (birth of the first child, college life, marriage, death of a parent, etc.). Collectives and communities behave much the same way. Their anchors are changed by significant world and cultural events (World War II, 9/11, COVID, the Beatles, etc.). In my case, many ideas that were once core to my belief systems were replaced by experiences of travel, trauma, and love.

As a child of generational trauma, perhaps my anchors were not set as deeply within my psyche. Perhaps, in fact, they were ill-formed when I met my wife and began my journey toward her culture. Or perhaps I was just blessed to experience so much. Looking back now,

I can see that an abundant universe sent the forces of heaven and humanity to pick me up. I can't begin to name all the people and the organizations that eventually came to my aid. But if I refuse to credit them, I break the Law of Jante: "Don't convince yourself that you are better than us."[74]

And that is the lesson of Jante—be grateful and dare to see grace in your journey as a willfully dependent member of your community. It's OK to be proud of one's accomplishments or, more specifically, of the accomplishments of one's community and one's citizenship in that community. But be weary when congratulating yourself for self-reliance. Or judging yourself or others on the absence of it. It may blind us to the community that actually did pick us up or, worse, to what is truly alive in them or us. It is in this willful interdependence that I am, in fact, proud. The point of sharing my story is not to demonstrate an individual pride that would break the Law of Jante but to demonstrate and defend a different kind of pride, one in us.

Children should not need to find their own bootstraps, and when they do, they should keep sight of the village that also lifted them up. They should remember where they came from, and if not simply for further transcendence, they should be grateful. Gratitude is the key to transcendence.

> **WE DO NOT SEE THINGS AS THEY ARE. WE SEE THINGS AS WE ARE.**
> **—RABBI SHEMUEL BEN NACHMANI, AS QUOTED IN THE TALMUDIC TRACTATE BERAKHOT**

The rise of Teal and evolutionary organizations has essential implications for the future of work, communities, and organizations.

It is my firm belief that these movements will gain momentum as more millennials take over leadership and more Gen Z enters the workplace. As more and more communities adopt these holistic and self-managing structures, we can expect to see a shift toward environments that are more flexible, collaborative, and empowering. This will require a new approach to leadership, one that is focused on supporting and enabling people to support and enable each other.

I want to argue abundance for the entire array of human needs. This argument may land more naturally to people who have found sources of abundance or for those who put their faith in higher powers, be it a deity or the natural world, and, in doing so, reject materialism and scarcity. I certainly know that people on our planet still starve to death, so I understand how ridiculous it may be to argue that food is not scarce for anyone. I would say that more food is hoarded, withheld, or thrown away in the world than is needed.

I also argue that *human beings have an unlimited capacity to feed one another and, in doing so, to heal themselves.* But throughout history, toxic collectives have fabricated malevolent ghosts to garner power and hoard resources. This, then, is my idea of evil: refusing to feed another human, labeling their appetite for love and belonging as unworthy, and withholding esteem, equality, and interdependence.

Many leaders of organizations today are realizing that we are spiritual creatures, and try as we may to put this aside for the sake of unity, we injure ourselves because our spirituality can be the most unifying of needs. Spirituality reflects what is alive in us and, in doing so, unites us as a species. It is a deep-seated yearning to attach with others, to something greater than ourselves, and to find meaning and purpose in our lives. This need is shared by people of all cultures, backgrounds, and beliefs, and it is a fundamental part of what makes us human.

As I previously shared, Frederic Laloux, in his book *Reinventing Organizations*, argues that spirituality is a critical component of healthy and effective organizations.[75] He suggests that by tapping into our spiritual needs, we can create more harmonious and productive work environments.[76] Maslow's hierarchy of needs also recognizes the importance of spirituality in achieving self-actualization. He believed that once our basic physiological and safety needs are met, we have a natural drive to seek spiritual fulfillment. Rosenberg gave us the language to attach nonviolently, without judgment and feed our needs and one another's.

Early in this book, I mentioned that our lives and anxieties are like a tangled fishing line. The more we rush to "pull on the line," to hastily judge others, and to allow perceived judgments to influence us, the tighter we pull these emotional knots. We quickly develop triggers that act like new tangles and, when force is applied, quickly become new knots. And like a nylon fishing line, once a knot is removed, the line still retains the memory of the knot, and it's easier for knots to reform quickly. Like a violent response to a tangled line, violent communication, which was much of the topic of this book, creates knots from simple tangles and draws conflict based on the judgment of ourselves and others.

Identities matter. I discussed how I developed my first positive self-identities in the eleventh grade. I mentioned how my uniforms made me feel that I belonged and how I had to find validation for my esteem, both externally and internally. I told you how, as my identity developed, it seemed to threaten my mother and how that meant I had to leave home at seventeen to unfold my identity. Our identities are the most important thing we own and extend into the world. They are ours, and no one should seek to hold them hostage or inhibit the authentic free expression of self-actualization, not even schools, churches, managers, or parents.

The famous economist John Maynard Keynes wrote during the great depression in 1930 that in 2030, the world would know an abundance that would "solve the economic problem."[77] The vision he had was that technology would multiply the productivity of human beings to such an extent that we would be able to choose to work fifteen hours a week and spend most of our time on leisure and higher-level pursuits (self-actualization). Critics of this worldview say that Keynes underestimated humanity's need to work and that consumers just started consuming more. I think these critics are not entirely incorrect and that much of the division and toxicity in our society is the handling of this "economic problem."

Should we consume ever more and grow economies ever faster? Is that a sustainable worldview? Does sustainability even matter?

An abundance of resources has emerged, but most have chosen to consume and hoard more. I also posit that much of this is just a tangled fishing line on the bottom of our boat. We consume out of a competitive spirit in order to "keep up with the Joneses." We act to avoid the humiliation of defeat in a world that sees labels like winners and losers through masks of inauthenticity. We do not allow ourselves the time or space to clean up the knots, so our lines do not leave the boat any longer.

We become extrinsic in nature because we have little connection to the intrinsic, what is actually alive in us. Many who will have fond memories of nature trips as youth will abandon such ambitions for material consumption, which is a quick fix. Modern marketing techniques have thus far convinced us that new "needs" emerge, we must have a new car every two years, we need to the latest fashion, and so on, and to keep up with the metaphorical "Joneses," we must then continue to work more and harder to get ahead and "win." The Joneses, after all, do not take vacations, do they? Losers take vacations?

I recall the time my junior high daughter came home from her Norwegian school, letting me know her teacher had excused her from the study of algebra. I remember the conversation well when I told my fourteen-year-old daughter that artists often needed a backup plan. That if she wanted to support a family, she would need one. I was so disappointed in her teacher's naïve exploration of my child's organic calling.

The response I got from Katherine was priceless. Honestly, while I was not ready to hear this, I am still in awe. "Dad," she said, "I don't care about money. I want to be an artist." She was connected with what was alive in her; her fishing line was solidly in the water with no tangles. And yet I, as a parent, was encouraging her to pull on the line; I was the source of the tangles and knots.

> **SOMEDAY, I HOPE I CAN GROW UP TO BE MY FOURTEEN-YEAR-OLD DAUGHTER.**

Keynes may be more correct than we thought. As we see the rise of artificial intelligence (AI) and machines exceedingly able to replace human functions (yes, even algebra), I see a world where authentic human inspiration is the only precious thing. As an entrepreneur and CEO, I recognized that my inspiration, the ideas that moved the ball exponentially, is always a product of a good vacation and time in Norway. It is when I take time daily and seasonally to manage the tangles and knots that I can sense what is alive in me and what the universe or God is speaking into me.

My home state of California has started this year to fund prekindergarten programs for "students" as young as three years old. This is amazing, in that it allows otherwise homebound parents (often mothers) the opportunity to return to their careers sooner.

In Norway, it is standard for the taxpayer to help fund childcare so that young families, especially moms, get back into the workplace. However, they do not attempt to call it an educational investment. I admire that Norwegians do not try to "educate" children before six or seven years old. There is a season where we need to let kids be kids, to connect to themselves and others without judgments and assessments.

Before the age of six, Norwegian kids learn to climb rocks and trees, navigate playground rules, attach to nonfamilial gratification sources (including nature), and have a social life outside the home. I sincerely hope that American parents are not tossing their prekindergarten children into a pipeline of education designed to tie their lines in knots, to make them better at algebra, but to be more judgmental, competitive, violent, and less creative. This would be a pipeline that ends only after graduate school when they enter the workplace to compete with AI and machines.

I sense a future where Keynes is half correct. Some of our children will participate in a "sweat economy"[78] based on their ability to perform calculations, solve complex problems, perform advanced laboratory work, climb ladders, and so on. But by then, machines will also be capable of doing everything they have learned since they gave up climbing trees at four years old. The alternative is a portion of society that fulfills Keynes's prediction; these are people like my wonderful daughter, who heeded another strategy or were raised differently. They instead were encouraged to look within for their actual and organic nature; they unfolded what their heart had for the universe.

These people will work less simply because their work demands inspiration. This I will call the "inspiration economy," people who work less simply because their "work" is play, organic expression from a place of spiritual centeredness. This perhaps is the fifteen-hour workweek.

Others may feel threatened by this value set and judge it falsely. From a scarcity perspective, they will argue that success is still defined by how much we accumulate. They will justify this to themselves to return to the offices and work even more hours. The idea that we would work less and consume less to be *more spiritually present* is not at odds with the idea that others would be *more materially focused and productive*.

What we have learned at Agile Six is not only that these things are seasonal and needs-based but also that in an age where more productivity can be defined spiritually and heuristically and not algorithmically, and when AI and machines are emerging to replace "hard work," value is increasingly the product of inspiration, of balance, and of love and presence.

The nonviolent leader needs to be aware of this change; they need to be able to:

- speak the NVC language of all levels to all identities.

- understand how identities form (both for collectives and for individuals) based on Maslow's hierarchy of needs and advocate for them.

- feed and teach feeding of needs to individual and collective identities with abundance.

- reject the fallacies of scarcity-based binary arguments or value judgments.

- manage individual egos (of themselves, individuals, and collective identities).

- push identities toward abundance while not judging those who move slower.

- create healthy belonging through truly inclusive practices.

- at every opportunity, find an argument for abundance.

- resist and dismantle inequities and paternalism.

- actively promote and model rest, regeneration, and inspiration.

- listen to the universe from a place of rest (sense and respond).

- embrace emergent strategy to respond.

- be authentically and compassionately themselves.

WHAT DO I HOPE I HAVE ACHIEVED WITH THIS BOOK?

Let me restate this from chapter 1. First, *bet the whole enchilada on people.* Stop pulling on the line. Trust people, and they will be trustworthy. Believe in them, and they will believe in themselves, put purpose before profit, and see how it maximizes both. Mind the lines for tangles and practice NVC. As you do, you will attract like-minded soulmates and feed their souls and families. Model balance and take vacations, and demand that others do so as well. Hold space for emergence, unfolding, and dreaming; these things cannot manifest in unbalanced or violent workplaces. *Be vulnerable and love people, and they will do the same.* This is leadership.

Second, *expect more from your politicians, employers, and one another.* Accept nothing less than trust, purpose, autonomy, and wholeness. You can stop the cycle of judgments and ask for balance. If you want to realize your full potential, you must demand nothing less. You should be welcome to bring the fullness of your identity or all you are comfortable bringing to work. You should be able to express your humanity and unfold it, bring it home whole, and have the energy to share it even more with your family. This is the world we need to build; it is then the world *we need to demand*. Trust me—I did, and it made all the difference.

Finally, *embrace your countrymen as interdependent compatriots*. End the culture war. We have defined our culture as one of independence and freedom. But this is simply a cowboy fairytale. We swim in the same waters, we thrive in the same economy, we breathe the same air, and our grandchildren will suffer the same consequences of our division and individualism. *That starts with willful and proud ownership of our interdependence*. A true patriot loves their country and their countrymen.

Now, more than ever, the world needs a new kind of leader who sees abundance and not scarcity, takes risks to question their conceptions, and dares to talk of love, belonging, esteem, wholeness, and transcendence. We desperately need these leaders in our government, classrooms, communities, and businesses to see what unites us, what is alive in us, and what needs to be unfolded, not tangled up.

ABOUT THE AUTHOR

Robert Rasmussen has been honored to represent some of the world's best companies and to lead and be led by some of the world's most talented people. He has served world-class technology teams in the U.S., Norway, Sweden, Denmark, Finland, Belgium, Netherlands, Lithuania, Estonia, and virtually.

A service-disabled Veteran of the U.S. Navy, he is the cofounder and CEO of Agile Six, a company that helps government agencies create customized digital solutions to meet their users' needs. He also founded the Digital Services Coalition, a group of over forty like-minded firms working together to accelerate the government's ability to implement services focusing on good usability, reliable technology, and accessibility for all.

Robert enjoys travel, fishing, boating, scuba diving, and writing in his spare time.

VISIT HIS BLOG AT WWW.BETTERPLACES.BLOG FOR MORE ENGAGING STORIES AND INSIGHTS ON CREATING BETTER PLACES.

ENDNOTES

1   Marshall B. Rosenberg and Deepak Chopra, Nonviolent Communication: *A Language of Life: Life-Changing Tools for Healthy Relationships*, 3rd ed. (Encinitas, CA: PuddleDancer Press, 2015).

2   Ibid.

3   Bill Cosby, "A quote by Bill Cosby," Goodreads, accessed April 3, 2024, https://www.goodreads.com/quotes/207179-i-brought-you-in-this-world-and-i-can-take.

4   Abraham H. Maslow, *The Farther Reaches of Human Nature* (New York: Penguin Books, 1993).

5   Scott Barry Kaufman, *Transcend: The New Science of Self-Actualization* (New York: TarcherPerigee, 2020), 31.

6   "World happiness, trust, and social connections in times of crisis," The World Happiness Report, March 20, 2023, https://worldhappiness.report/ed/2023/world-happiness-trust-and-social-connections-in-times-of-crisis/.

7   "VAT rates in Denmark," Marosavat.com, accessed April 7, 2024, https://marosavat.com/vat/denmark/#:~:text=VAT%20rates%20in%20Denmark%20by,0%25%20VAT%20rate%20is%20provided.

8   Ibid.

9   Meik Wiking, *The Little Book of Hygge: The Danish Way to Live Well* (London: Penguin Life, 2016), 6.

10 Ibid., 282.

11 Aksel Sandemose, *A Fugitive Crosses His Tracks*, trans. Eugene Gay-Tifft (New York: A.A. Knopf, 1936), 77.

12 President George W. Bush, "Address to a joint session of congress and the American people,'" September 20, 2001, https://georgewbush-whitehouse.archives.gov/news/releases/2001/09/20010920-8.html.

13 "10 Years commemoration of 22 July – speech by NATO Secretary General Jens Stoltenberg," NATO, accessed April 7, 2024, https://www.nato.int/cps/en/natohq/opinions_185902.htm.

14 Mark E. Koltko-Rivera, "Rediscovering the Later Version of Maslow's Hierarchy of Needs: Self-Transcendence and Opportunities for Theory, Research, and Unification," *Review of General Psychology* 10, no. 4 (2006): 302–317, https://doi.org/10.1037/1089-2680.10.4.302.

15 Abraham H. Maslow, "Various Meanings of Transcendence," *Journal of Transpersonal Psychology* 1 (1969): 56–66.

16 Ibid.

17 Shawn Achor, "The Happiness Advantage: The Seven Principles of Positive Psychology That Fuel Success and Performance at Work," *Choice Reviews Online* 48, no.07 (2011): 48–4166, https://doi.org/10.5860/choice.48-4166.

18 Shawn Achor, *The Happiness Advantage: The Seven Principles of Positive Psychology That Fuel Success and Performance at Work* (New York: Crown Business, 2010), 15.

19 Marcus Buckingham, *First, Break All the Rules: What the World's Greatest Managers Do Differently* (New York: Simon & Schuster, 1999).

20 Frederic Laloux, *Reinventing Organizations: A Guide to Creating Organizations Inspired by the Next Stage in Human Consciousness* (Millis, MA: Nelson Parker, 2014).

21 Ibid.

22 Ibid., 55–56.

23 Ibid., 44.

24 Ibid., 40.

25 Ibid., 38.

26 Ibid., 36.

27 "Trauma-aware definition," Attachment & Trauma Network, Inc., January 6, 2024, accessed April 1, 2024, https://www.attachment-traumanetwork.org/trauma-aware-definition/.

28 Nicole Baumer and Julia Frueh, "What Is Neurodiversity?," Harvard Health Blog, Harvard Health Publishing, November 23, 2021, https://www.health.harvard.edu/blog/what-is-neurodiversity-202111232645.

29 "State of Gen Z mental health," Harmony Healthcare IT, accessed April 1, 2024, https://www.harmonyhit.com/state-of-gen-z-mental-health/.

30 Sophie Bethune, "Gen Z more likely to report mental health concerns," Monitor on Psychology, American Psychological Association, January 1, 2019, https://www.apa.org/monitor/2019/01/gen-z.

31 "New ZenBusiness research finds class of 2023 sees neurodiversity as an asset in leadership, is primed to be the most entrepreneurial," Business Wire, June 14, 2023, https://www.businesswire.com/news/home/20230614082058/en/New-ZenBusiness-Research-Finds-Class-of-2023-Sees-Neurodiversity-as-an-Asset-in-Leadership-is-Primed-to-be-the-Most-Entrepreneurial.

32 Ibid.

33 "About," Evelin Lindner, accessed April 1, 2024, https://www.humili-ationstudies.org/whoweare/evelin.php.

34 Evelin Gerda Lindner, "In Times of globalization and human rights: does humiliation become the most disruptive force?," *Journal of Human Dignity and Humiliation Studies* 1, no. 1 (March 2007), http://www.humilliationstudies.upeace.org/.

35 Michael C. Bender, "Trump calls some unauthorized immigrants 'animals' in rant," *The New York Times*, May 16, 2018, https://www.nytimes.com/2018/05/16/us/politics/trump-undocumented-immi-grants-animals.html.

36 Amy Chozick, "Hillary Clinton calls many Trump backers 'deplora-bles,' and G.O.P. pounces," *The New York Times*, September 10, 2016, https://www.nytimes.com/2016/09/11/us/politics/hillary-clinton-basket-of-deplorables.html.

37 Jeffrey Herf, *The Jewish Enemy: Nazi Propaganda During World War II and the Holocaust* (Cambridge, MA: Harvard University Press, 2006), 14.

38 Samantha Power, *A Problem from Hell: America and the Age of Genocide* (New York: Basic Books, 2002), 338.

39 United States Holocaust Memorial Museum, "Treaty of Versailles," accessed April 8, 2024, https://encyclopedia.ushmm.org/content/en/article/treaty-of-versailles#:~:text=The%20shame%20of%20defeat%20and,war%E2%80%9D%20just%2020%20years%20later.&text=The%20treaty%20required%20demilitarization%20of,extensive%20reparation%20payments%20by%20Germany.

40 Bono, *Surrender: 40 Songs, One Story* (New York: Alfred A. Knopf, 2022).

41   Ibid.

42   Theodore Roosevelt, *The Naval War of 1812* (New York: G.P. Putnam's Sons, 1882), 228.

43   Ibid.

44   "The preamble," National Constitution Center, accessed April 3, 2024, https://constitutioncenter.org/the-constitution/preamble/interpretations/37.

45   Mark Twain, *The Innocents Abroad* (Hartford, CT: American Publishing Company, 1869).

46   Ibid.

47   George Washington, "Washington's farewell address to the people of the United States," Founders Online, National Archives, September 19, 1796, https://founders.archives.gov/documents/Washington/05-20-02-0440-0002.

48   "U.S. spending on it products, services, and staff 2012-2022," Statista, July 7, 2023, https://www.statista.com/statistics/821769/us-spending-it-products-services-staff/#:~:text=The%20U.S.%20spending%20on%20technology,(COVID-19)%20pandemic.

49   "The United States spends more on defense than the next 10 countries combined," Peter G. Peterson Foundation, April 20, 2023, https://www.pgpf.org/blog/2023/04/the-united-states-spends-more-on-defense-than-the-next-10-countries-combined.

50   Ibid.

51   Curtlyn Kramer, "Vital stats: businesspeople in congress," Brookings Institution, February 17, 2017, https://www.brookings.edu/articles/vital-stats-businesspeople-in-congress/.

52   Grace Dean, "Costco CEO says that only a 'really small percent' of members misuse their cards, 'but when you're dealing with 'millions of transactions' it adds up," Business Insider, June 9, 2023, https://www.businessinsider.com/costco-membership-cards-misuse-self-checkout-service-buy-pay-id-2023-6#:~:text=As%20of%20early%20May%2C%20Costco,imminent%20increase%20in%20membership%20fees.

53   "About Costco," Costco.com, accessed April 7, 2024, https://www.costco.com/about.html.

54   "Meet Costco's multimillionaire cofounder Jim Sinegal, a democrat Megadonor who was only paid a third of the average CEO's salary during his time leading the wholesale retailer," Business Insider, September 16, 2020, https://www.businessinsider.com/meet-costco-cofounder-jim-sinegal-net-worth-house-philanthropy-2020-9?op=1.

55   Dominic Rushe, "Martin Shkreli barred from drug industry and fined $64.6m by US Court," The Guardian, January 14, 2022, https://www.theguardian.com/us-news/2022/jan/14/martin-shkreli-barred-drug-industry-fined-us-court.

56   Romina Boccia and Dominik Lett, "Fast facts about discretionary spending," Cato Institute, accessed April 7, 2024, https://www.cato.org/blog/fast-facts-about-discretionary-spending.

57   Ibid.

58   Charles Ornstein, "Here's why Healthcare.gov broke down," ProPublica, February 14, 2020, https://www.propublica.org/article/heres-why-healthcaregov-broke-down.

59   Charlie Spiering, "Jon Stewart challenges Kathleen Sebelius on Obamacare individual mandate," Washington Examiner, October 8, 2013, https://www.washingtonexaminer.com/opinion/beltway-confidential/1169448/jon-stewart-challenges-kathleen-sebelius-on-obamacare-individual-mandate/.

60 "U.S. digital service," U.S. Digital Service, accessed April 7, 2024, https://www.usds.gov/.

61 "Day one: Mikey Dickerson, U.S. digital service administrator," The White House, August 20, 2014, https://obamawhitehouse.archives.gov/blog/2014/08/20/day-one-mikey-dickerson-us-digital-service-administrator.

62 "The U.S. digital services playbook," U.S. Digital Service, accessed April 7, 2024, https://playbook.cio.gov/.

63 Ibid.

64 "Transparency and open government," Federal Register, January 26, 2009, accessed April 7, 2024, https://www.federalregister.gov/documents/2009/01/26/E9-1777/transparency-and-open-government.

65 Abraham Lincoln, "The Gettysburg address," delivered November 19, 1863, Gettysburg, Pennsylvania.

66 Jennifer Pahlka, "Coding a better government," TED, accessed April 7, 2024, https://www.ted.com/talks/jennifer_pahlka_coding_a_better_government.

67 "The Norwegian digitalisation agency," Government.no, accessed April 7, 2024, https://www.regjeringen.no/en/dep/dfd/org/etater-og-virksomheter-under-digitaliserings-og-forvaltningsdepartementet/underliggende-etater/digitaliseringsdirektoratet/id2684200/.

68 "Open government directive," The White House, accessed April 7, 2024, https://obamawhitehouse.archives.gov/open/documents/open-government-directive.

69 Jessica Mulholland, "What Obama did for Tech: USDS and 18F," GovTech, April 23, 2021, https://www.govtech.com/civic/what-obama-did-for-tech-usds-and-18f.html.

70 "Digital Services Coalition – mission," Digital Services Coalition, accessed April 3, 2024, https://digitalservicescoalition.org/mission/.

71 Ibid.

72 Ibid.

73 Ibid.

74 Ibid.

75 Ibid.

76 Ibid.

77 Institute for the Future, "Looking 100 years into the future: lessons from John Maynard Keynes," accessed April 4, 2024, https://legacy.iftf.org/future-now/article-detail/looking-100-years-into-the-future-lessons-from-john-maynard-keynes/.

78 Ibid.

www.ingramcontent.com/pod-product-compliance
Lightning Source LLC
Chambersburg PA
CBHW031431270326
41930CB00007B/655